APPRAISING PERSONALITY

AN INTRODUCTION TO
THE PROJECTIVE TECHNIQUES

by Molly Harrower, Ph.D.

A CLARION BOOK
PUBLISHED BY SIMON AND SCHUSTER

To C.C.S. AND L.S.K.

A CLARION BOOK
PUBLISHED BY SIMON AND SCHUSTER
ROCKEFELLER CENTER, 630 FIFTH AVENUE
NEW YORK, NEW YORK 10020

FIRST PAPERBACK PRINTING 1968

MANUFACTURED IN THE UNITED STATES OF AMERICA
PRINTED BY MURRAY PRINTING CO., FORGE VILLAGE, MASS.
BOUND BY ELECTRONIC PERFECT BINDERS, INC., BROOKLYN, N.Y.

Contents

List of Illustrations

Introduction to the First Edition

Among the various potentialities of psychology in its relatively rapid growth during the past fifty years there appeared the possibility that by means of large collections of careful observations of human performance, types or classes of persons could be recognized and described. Long, long before the twentieth century, practical experience had shown that there are different kinds of people. But since there were also different kinds of observers, the question remained for the psychologists as to whether tests could be devised that would have predictive value, i.e., that would not only describe different kinds of people but would do so in ways that would permit a fairly reliable forecast of their future attitudes and behavior. Some few psychologists, at the risk of their colleagues' disapproval, addressed themselves to the immensely difficult task of devising objective and definable tests that would sort out individuals into distinguishable groups, even though the boundary lines might well await more precise definition. In short, psychologists began to apply what they had learned and to refine their assumptions in actual experience. Working at the fringes of knowledge requires courage, for it is unconventional as well as hazardous. But by now, clinical psychologists have found procedures of real value to doctors.

The doctor's primary task is to determine what is the disease that afflicts his patient. But on many occasions, and certainly for planning the care of the patient, it is almost equally important to find out as early as can be what kind of a person he is dealing with. The assumption that this latter task may best be left to the doctor's intuition, or innate sagacity, or long experience, simply begs the question of the importance of the knowledge of personality in the practice of medicine. Experience has already shown that deliberate study of the methods of appraising personality reveals a great deal that is of value to the doctor. The scientist's purpose is to approximate ever more closely the actual state of affairs. Like all other sciences, psychology is in a state of becoming — not being. Among other things, it is becoming more accurate and more dependable. No one could claim finality or perfection for the theories or practices of clinical psychologists. But it is vain to deny that they are concerned with something of intimate and enduring value to the practice of medicine — the appraisal of personality. And they are furthering our systematic and useful knowledge.

This book offers to the reader a glimpse of some of the present methods and some of the problems of the clinical psychologist, and more than an introduction to the potential value of psychological tests in the practice of medicine. In its style it invites, and in its content it deserves, the attention of those who like to comb the unfamiliar to remove the burrs of misunderstanding and ignorance.

Alan Gregg, M.D.

April 10, 1952

Preface to the Second Edition

This book was originally written with the physician in mind. It grew out of questions actually raised by a group of army doctors taking a course in psychotherapeutic medicine organized by the Surgeon-General's office. Its aim was to alert the medical man to a potential collaborator on psychosomatic problems, namely, the clinical psychologist using the projective techniques.

At that time, it is true, we expected other ancillary professions — social workers, clergymen, lawyers, teachers, counselors, nurses, and the alert layman — to be interested. In this we were not disappointed for some of the most favorable reviews were found in periodicals in the social sciences.

Interestingly enough, however, it has proved over the years that for every physician or social scientist who became interested in the book there were twenty beginning students in psychology who sought it out as an orientation to more systematic and detailed study of the projectives. Beginning psychology students have "petitioned" that the book again be readily available for introductory courses.

In undertaking a revision, therefore, it has been with the "would-be" psychology student in mind. This being the case it might have seemed a simple matter to underscore the change in emphasis by putting the questions in the mouths of the students rather than the physician. Funnily enough, when this was attempted with some classes, it seemed less effective as a teaching device. Somehow — in line with a good projective principle — the resistances of psychology students seemed more easily overcome when the "other fellow," the "medic," asked the questions! For the main part of the discussion, therefore, we have left the physician as the devil's advocate, displaying his ignorance and groping for understanding.

In the interests of a more complete volume, we have added a chapter, "Some Truths From Tall Tales," relating to the Thematic Apperception Test and additional case histories in Part III.

It must be emphasized, as in the first edition, that this is not a textbook. We have attempted no comprehensive survey of the ever-growing literature in this field. We expect the student, the "would-be" clinical psychologist, ultimately to become well grounded in his own right in the technical details of the methods and procedures which are discussed here. Our hope is to give him a *meaningful first exposure* to the projectives.

As far as the physician is concerned, our aim is to give him a "feel" of the raw material with which the psychologist deals, and from which he derives his conclusions and frames his reports. We want to show the physician the kind of question he is entitled to ask of those who handle the new tools in clinical psychology. In the days of the family doctor, and in those communities where this pattern still exists, the patient's background and history are personally known to the physician, and the psychological appraisal, even if available, would be less important. The majority of physicians, particularly in cities, meet their patients as comparative strangers. If properly presented, findings of the psychological tests of the present day can do something toward providing the same type of information which was previously assimilated unconsciously by the family physician, as a result of his opportunities to see his patient in various interpersonal relationships over a period of time.

In this book we have attempted to minimize technical language. If the main purpose is to communicate facts which are to be pertinent at an interdisciplinary level, then the finer nuances of the specialist's language can well be sacrificed, for, by definition, the "specialist" has restricted his field of communication.

In the first part of this book, the questions most often asked by "would-be" psychologists and by physicians have been dealt with. What does a clinical psychologist do? What are these projective techniques? What kind of information do the tests reveal? How reliable are they? Can psychologists be wrong? Is anyone normal? Must many tests be given to evaluate a patient? Are some better than others? Are my own answers really revealing?

In Part II, some of the well-known psychological tests have been discussed with the "raw material" derived from patients with various types of disturbances as examples. It is hoped that this "raw material," the substance of the patient's productions, will have increasing meaning in and of itself for the physician if he meets up with it in psychological reports.

In Part III, the case histories are presented together with

the psychologist's report. Here we want to show the kind of information made available to the physician through the battery of tests in supplementation of his own findings. By this time we hope that the reader, a psychology student, a physician, or an interested layman would have a general idea of the significance of the type of test (Part I) and a specific idea of the material provided by the patient (Part II), so that these reports will not be seen as authoritative or somewhat arbitrary pronouncements, but as the clinical psychologist's ideas and conclusions based on the material which the patient provides. No psychological report is ever all-inclusive. It is valuable insofar as it contributes relevant material to the particular problem under consideration by the physician.

Throughout Parts I and II, the dialogue has been adopted as a vehicle for the discussion, and we have included several charts so as to introduce a visual type of survey, which we believe affords a convenient way of interpatient comparison. In Part III the exchange of hypothetical letters between the physician and the psychologist accompanies actual case histories and the actual reports which accompanied them. In some instances, it has been necessary to adopt minor changes to avoid disclosure of a patient's identity.

Molly Harrower, Ph.D.

January, 1964

PART ONE

[I]

~~~~~~~~~~~~~~~~~~~~~~~~~~~~~~~~~~~~~~

What Does the Clinical
Psychologist Do?

As a general introduction of the field of Clinical Psychology, we may imagine a conversation between classmates at a twentieth reunion. Robert Jones, M.D., and John Smith, Ph.D., despite living in the same town rarely meet. Jones, a general practitioner, starts the conversation in an attempt to catch up on this "new-fangled profession of clinical psychology" which he has been hearing about from some of his patients.

Physician: Hi, Smith — you're just the fellow I've been looking for. Heard of you from one of my patients the other day. Said she'd been to see you for some examination or other. What are you doing? You'd better bring my scanty knowledge of psychology up to date; from the little I took in college, I can't see any connection between its subject matter and the troubles of my hypertensive patient.

Psychologist: I can see what you mean. But academic psychology of 30 years ago was concerned with a totally different field of investigation and body of knowledge from what we now, as clinical psychologists, are interested in. Running rats through mazes, which you and I did in the old lab, differentiating between various degrees of brightness in experiments on visual acuity, demonstrating the size-weight illusion, learning nonsense syllables to demonstrate the laws of retention and recall — these admittedly are a far cry from the emotional problems with which we now deal professionally.

Physician: Glad to hear you say so. I was feeling baffled. Tell me, just what is this "clinical" psychology that you talk about?

Psychologist: The new profession of clinical psychology is slowly emerging as a recognized sociological entity, although the term was introduced as far back as 1896. It's a new job, created by the utilizing of new tools in dealing with human problems. We are only just beginning, amongst ourselves, to define our professional duties satisfactorily, to outline the training which we feel should be required of those who enter the profession, and to draw up an ethical code under the terms of which we will function. However, individual clinical psychologists have been working long enough and in enough places to have become part of the local framework of facilities available to persons in psychological distress, so I can give you a general picture of our activities.

Physician: I'm interested in that. In what way do you function in the assistance of the mentally disturbed? Is your province similar to that of a psychiatrist? Do you treat people or only examine them?

Psychologist: Let me begin at the beginning. I will talk about a hypothetical person, a composite picture of several of us who have gone into this field. A clinical psychologist gets his Doctor's degree in some branch of psychology. His basic, intensive, scientific training is not, as is yours or that of our psychiatric colleagues, in the field of the medical sciences. In addition to his major work in psychology, in all probability, he will have done work in some allied field such as sociology, anthropology, and philosophy. Then he will have spent some additional years in the study of the specific tools, methods, and ways of investigating human personality. These methods have become known as the "projective techniques" and they are the instruments by which the psychologist provides information on the underlying motivations of the individuals he investigates. At the same time, he may have undergone a personal analysis and spent one or two years in close collaboration with his medical colleagues, either as an intern in some psychiatric or neurological hospital or in a clinic or guidance center where he will have an opportunity to relate his findings to the medical and psychiatric evaluation of the case.

Physician: Well and good, but I have a very concrete mind. I understand things better if I am presented with actual examples. Tell me about some of the patients you see, the reasons why they are sent to you, and in general what sort of things you can tell about them.

Psychologist: Well, that shouldn't be too difficult. Let me see — on Monday I spent the day testing a boy in his second year of medical school who had suddenly begun to do very badly in his studies.

Physician: You only saw one patient?

Psychologist: Sounds strange, I know, and it often surprises people because they do not realize how time-consuming the evaluation of the psychological material can be.

Physician: Do the tests take long to give?

Psychologist: The actual testing is not the most time-consuming thing. But the test material, when it has been accumulated, has to be evaluated and interpreted, and a report has to be written which gives relevant information to the referring physician. Testing two patients and writing two full reports would be a pretty heavy day's work. One could, of course, test several patients and write the reports at another time, but one has to allow from three to five hours for each case that is adequately tested, worked up and reported on.

Physician: Sorry I interrupted you. You were telling me about the young medical student.

Psychologist: Yes, it's a rather interesting case. He comes from a well-known family and was, you might say, all set for a brilliant career. When he began to do badly, there were enough persons with psychiatric orientation in his family so that he came very soon under the care of one of the best psychiatrists in the city, largely to discover whether or not some emotional disturbance was the cause of his sudden failure. The psychiatrist who was examining him, however, did not find any of the symptoms which might have been expected. He was referred for examination for whatever light could be thrown on his case by our test findings. In this instance, the psychological findings were very startling.

Physician: What did you find from the tests?

Psychologist: We strongly suspected from the findings that the boy's trouble arose from the fact that he had a slow-growing brain tumor, which, while it did not impair his overall intelligence, was affecting his creative thinking, his productiveness, and his capacity for abstraction to a marked degree.

Physician: You can tell that he has a brain tumor from your tests?

Psychologist: It is not quite as direct as that. We cannot tell with one hundred per cent certainty that he has a brain tumor. What we can point to is that some specific functions have been, as it were, knocked out, leaving others intact. The personality had acquired a stereotyped character, an impoverishment, a restriction of the psychological horizons which we have found to exist in patients with specific organic defects of the brain verified at operation. In this instance, my suggestion was, of course, that an electroencephalogram be done. The findings confirmed my suspicions. Let's see, I have the report here:

"The electroencephalogram indicates that there is a focus of abnormally slow electrical activity appearing from the fronto-temporal region. This is regarded as presumptive evidence of a focal lesion in that region, most likely a brain tumor."

Physician: Is that something which frequently happens in your practice? Surely not!

Psychologist: No, as a matter of fact, this finding is perhaps one in a thousand cases. However, a psychologist working in a neurological ward comes across this type of psychological finding frequently. In the ordinary run-of-the-mill of general practice, it is naturally very unusual.

Physician: What would have happened had there been no psychological examination?

Psychologist: Don't get the feeling that I consider myself indispensable in this connection. In this instance, however, it might have been easy to have overplayed the idea that some psychological disturbance was at the root of his trouble. This boy might have been put in treatment with some therapist on the assumption that his difficulties were basically emotional. He probably had emotional difficulties, as who does not? But I think the psychological tests may have saved considerable time since they highlighted so clearly that some organic condition was present.

Physician: Can you tell me what sort of things the test record, as you call it, of this boy showed?

Psychologist: It would take too long at this point, old man; if you were really interested, perhaps you could drop into my office sometime and I could show you some of the test material itself and tell you about it. The kind of technicality I could give you now would be meaningless, since you wouldn't have the background. However, I can show you a little chart that I use to summarize the test findings, which I think makes sense even if you don't know the tests themselves. [Smith takes a pad from his pocket on which is printed a chart entitled, SUMMARY OF TEST FINDINGS. He marks it up with a heavy pencil in the way that is shown in Chart 1.] I have devised this chart so that it would be possible for the physician to get a bird's-eye-view of how a patient reacted even though he does not know anything about the tests in detail. For example, take line one which describes in very general terms how the patient behaves during the tests. The boy I am talking about was

Chart I
Student with Brain Tumor
SUMMARY OF TEST FINDINGS

MANNER DURING TEST

| Overtly Distressed | **Uneasy** | Relaxed, Interested | Competitive and Tense | Hostile |

RATE OF PERFORMANCE

| Very Slow | **Slow** | Average | Speedy | Excessively Speedy |

I.Q. (BELLEVUE-WECHSLER)

| Below Average | Average | High Average | Superior | **Very Superior** |

PRODUCTIVITY (RORSCHACH)

| **Meager** | Average | Rich and well ordered | Rich, but chaotic | Chaotic |

RELATION TO REALITY
(RORSCHACH, BELLEVUE-WECHSLER, DRAWINGS)

| Fanatical exactitude | **Not noticeably disturbed** | Firm and good | "Artistic leeway" | Loose |

USUAL — UNUSUAL THOUGHT CONTENT
(RORSCHACH, UNPLEASANT CONCEPT)

| **Stereotyped** | Average | Original | Bizarre Qualities offset by other features | Bizarre |

EMOTIONAL TONE (RORSCHACH, SZONDI)

| Lacking, repressed | **Struggling for expression** | Warm, readily available | Getting out of hand | Emotions rampant |

CONSTRUCTIVE FANTASY (RORSCHACH)

| **Absent** | Average | Active | Active + | Topheavy, withdrawal |

PASSIVITY — AGGRESSION
(RORSCHACH, SZONDI, UNPLEASANT CONCEPT)

| Hampering passivity | **Insufficient drive** | Sufficient drive | Aggression + | Overpowering aggression |

somewhat *"uneasy."* Patients who cry during the interview or whose anxiety overpowers them would have been recorded as *"overtly distressed."* At the other end of the scale would be the hostile patient who resents having to be tested and is angry at the examiner.

Then it is important to know about the *Rate of Performance* — how quickly does the person respond, how much does he deviate from the average, are there any unusual delays? It has been found that the individual whose responses come much quicker than the average is disturbed in a different way from the patient whose replies or responses are very slow. The patient I am now describing was slower than the average.

The next line relates to the findings from a standard intelligence test. Here the range is from the *"low average"* up to *"very superior."* In this instance, our patient was found to have an I.Q. which fell in the Very Superior Group of the total population. This finding is important in the total diagnostic picture for some types of functions have been very well retained while others have been damaged.

The next line relates to the patient's productiveness, that is, in the same sense of his flow of spontaneous responses in one of the tests. This ranges from a *"meager"* flow, on the one hand, to one which is rich and well-ordered or, and again in contrast, to one that is a chaotic production that has lost its richness. This will become more understandable to you as you are introduced in detail to one of the tests, the Rorschach inkblot test.

Our patient, in this instance, has a very *meager* stream of associations. This despite the fact that he is very intelligent.

The line which is headed *Relation to Reality* will also become more meaningful to you when the tests themselves are explained. Let me at this moment give you a simple illustration. I will draw the letter "H" and ask you whether you will accept it as such. An individual whose relation to reality as shown in the tests is one of what I might call "fanatical exactitude" would not accept this as an "H" because there is a slight discrepancy in the length of the two parallel lines. An individual whose relation to reality is "not noticeably disturbed" or "firm and good" would, however, accept it. The individual whose test findings could be categorized as showing "artistic leeway" might say that this was not an "H" but a hurdle over which a runner had to jump. The individual, on the other hand, whose relationship to reality was "loose" might call this a dancing bear, that is, something with which (by all the ordinary laws of common sense) there appears to be no connection whatsoever.

In dealing with the line entitled *Usual or Unusual Thought Content*, we can see that there is the possibility of extremely original thoughts being contrasted with those that are bizarre or those which show no originality whatsoever. Here again this particular patient shows no originality in his thinking which is interesting when one compares it with the fact that he is someone of a very superior intelligence. In other words, his originality and his spontaneous productivity have suffered while he is still "very intelligent."

The line dealing with *Emotional Tone* varies again from the possibility of expressing a lack of emotion, on the one hand, to an overemphasis on the emotional aspects of life such that all else is obscured, on the other.

The line headed *Constructive Fantasy* allows us the possibility of appraising an individual who has retreated into his fantasy completely, the schizoid individual, whose fantasy is, therefore, "top-heavy" and shows withdrawal symptoms. At the other end we are able to record an individual who is deficient in imagination, and in this particular case, imagination is another of the faculties which has suffered.

The final line relates to the extent to which the individual is too passive or overpoweringly aggressive.

Physician: That was interesting. Let's hear about another case, one of your more usual ones this time.

Psychologist: Yesterday I saw a husband and wife. I have made it a rule when there are marital problems, and one member of the pair has consulted a psychiatrist or marriage counselor, not to make a report on the patient until I have also seen the partner's psychological test record.

Physician: You insist that they both be examined even if only one is sick?

Psychologist: Yes. It has proved time and time again that it is misleading to examine one member of a marital pair without the other. Or, let me say, the addition of the partner's record adds so much to one's understanding of the patient's problems, as to make it almost imperative to secure it.

Physician: What was the trouble in the case you are speaking of?

Psychologist: In this instance, Mr. X consulted the psychiatrist with a list of what appeared to be perfectly genuine complaints about his wife's behavior. The man was unusually intelligent and convincing in his description.

Moreover, when the psychiatrist had an interview with the wife, he found her to have many of the characteristics of immaturity and childishness which her husband had described and which he considered an impossible barrier to their adjustment. As a matter of fact, when I saw Mrs. X and her husband, my impressions were entirely those which had been elicited by psychiatric examination. However, and it is here that the tests play their vital contributing part, while it is true that Mrs. X appeared childish, anxious, overdependent, and emotionally immature on the tests which she took, and that her intelligence was a great deal lower than her husband's, as measured by our regular intelligence test scales — when her husband was examined, he proved, at the level to which the tests penetrate, to be much more seriously disturbed, although possessing an excellent facade or front. The husband, as a matter of fact, showed up to be a latent schizophrenic.

Physician: What were your suggestions then, in this case?

Psychologist: Well, it's quite obvious that merely treating the wife in an attempt to allay some of her anxiety and develop her to a point where she would have more independence and maturity would have been quite useless unless the husband, too, were treated. And, as a matter of fact, as you will realize, the handling of his case would require more time and would be a more difficult task since his difficulties lay at a deeper level. It is also possible to make the hypothesis that much of the anxiety exuded by the wife was a reaction to the more disturbed aspects of the husband's character, of which she was explicitly quite unaware.

Physician: Would you say that all the other problems handled in this way indicate disturbance in both parties, even if, on the face of it, one individual appeared completely "to blame"?

Psychologist: I certainly would not say that in every couple experiencing difficulties, one would prove to be a latent schizophrenic! On the other hand, as far as the tests are concerned, certain couples would appear to be virtually irreconcilable psychologically, since their emotional make-up seems utterly incompatible.

Physician: How about requiring psychological examinations of couples before marriage!

Psychologist: I doubt if one could *require* it! However, from the number of engaged couples who do come to get psychological appraisals of themselves, I am inclined to think that it is one of the most helpful and fruitful branches of our field of knowledge which has not yet been really fully explored.

Physician: Would it be possible to see how this couple looks on your chart?

Psychologist: Very easily. I will put them both on the same chart, boxing for Mr. X, and circling for Mrs. X. First, for the manner in which they undertook the examination. You will see that Mrs. X is uneasy and, at times, she cried a little. On the other hand, Mr. X goes at the tests in almost a competitive manner and shows, at times, some hostility to the examiner. You see, basically, he is insulted at the idea that he, too, has to be tested. Now look at the speed with which they each operate. Mrs. X is definitely slow; Mr. X is excessively speedy. And then look at their intelligence quotients. There is an enormous discrepancy here, with Mrs. X being slightly below average and Mr. X obtaining one of the highest scores possible. Now, let us turn to their productiveness. Again Mr. X would appear to have the richer psychological equipment, but this richness lacks order and at this point we begin to see some of Mr. X's difficulties. Take another important difference between them: their emotional responsiveness. Mrs. X is blocked but Mr. X proves to be much more emotionally disturbed than his appearance might suggest. There is also a significant feature of his thinking, namely, that there is a frankly bizarre quality to it.

From this chart, it is easy to see how fundamentally different these two individuals are: There is actually not a single area in which spontaneously they react in a similar way. Quite apart from the pathological findings in Mr. X's performance, that is, assuming there was no distortion of reality, one would still expect these two persons to have great difficulty in mutual adjustment. (Chart II)

Physician: This is beginning to make a little sense. Let's hear another case.

Psychologist: Well, offhand, I think of two individuals, both of whom were sent with almost identical notations by the physicians. In both cases, these individuals are described as extremely anxious, almost to the point of panic. One is afraid even to go out of the house alone. The other becomes overwhelmed with the fear that something will happen to her baby. Although these two patients present a somewhat similar picture clinically, that is, although as distressed people they appear to be very much alike in what they are suffering, the test findings are very different. In the one case, we are dealing with a strong, well-integrated personality who has momentarily been undergoing a period of acute stress, whereas in the other case, the whole "personality structure," as we call it, has been undermined and is on

Chart II
Mr. and Mrs. X
SUMMARY OF TEST FINDINGS

MANNER DURING TEST

Overtly Distressed	Uneasy	Relaxed, Interested	Competitive and Tense	Hostile

RATE OF PERFORMANCE

Very Slow	Slow	Average	Speedy	Excessively Speedy

I.Q. (BELLEVUE-WECHSLER)

Below Average	Average	High Average	Superior	Very Superior

PRODUCTIVITY (RORSCHACH)

Meager	Average	Rich and well ordered	Rich, but chaotic	Chaotic

RELATION TO REALITY
(RORSCHACH, BELLEVUE-WECHSLER, DRAWINGS)

Fanatical exactitude	Not noticeably disturbed	Firm and good	"Artistic leeway"	Loose

USUAL — UNUSUAL THOUGHT CONTENT
(RORSCHACH, UNPLEASANT CONCEPT)

Stereotyped	Average	Original	Bizarre Qualities offset by other features	Bizarre

EMOTIONAL TONE (RORSCHACH, SZONDI)

Lacking, repressed	Struggling for expression	Warm, readily available	Getting out of hand	Emotions rampant

CONSTRUCTIVE FANTASY (RORSCHACH)

Absent	Average	Active	Active +	Topheavy, withdrawal

PASSIVITY — AGGRESSION
(RORSCHACH, SZONDI, UNPLEASANT CONCEPT)

Hampering passivity	Insufficient drive	Sufficient drive	Aggression +	Overpowering aggression

the point of disintegrating or dissolving. In the case of the second patient, it was naturally my responsibility to point this out to the physician and to suggest that this patient should be handled in an institution rather than receiving help while attempting to carry on with her everyday life. In the case of the former, on the other hand, the test findings were encouraging and indicated that the anxiety was occurring in a personality with excellent intelligence and with an excellent capacity for creativeness and insight. There was nothing in the tests to indicate that the type of therapy which allows this patient to be confronted with some of her underlying problems should not be carried out. It was therefore suggested that she be referred to an analyst for treatment.

Physician: And how do these patients look on your chart?

Psychologist: I can show you very easily. I'll use the same device as before, boxing for one and circling for the other. You will see that their manner during the testing period is identical. They are both overtly distressed. Outside of that, however, they have nothing in common. Most of the circles fall in the central column for the better integrated patient, whereas the patient who is really disorganized by her anxiety shows up almost exclusively on the left-hand side of the chart. (Chart III)

Physician: Well, I'm beginning to think I could refer a case or two of my own to you. Give me one more.

Psychologist: Let's see what would be a good contrast. The other day I examined a man about to embark on analytic therapy. He has made up his mind to it, and the therapist has accepted him. What both of them are inter-

Chart III
Two "Anxious" Patients
SUMMARY OF TEST FINDINGS

MANNER DURING TEST

Overtly Distressed	Uneasy	Relaxed, Interested	Competitive and Tense	Hostile

RATE OF PERFORMANCE

Very Slow	Slow	Average	Speedy	Excessively Speedy

I.Q. (BELLEVUE-WECHSLER)

Below Average	Average	High Average	Superior	Very Superior

PRODUCTIVITY (RORSCHACH)

Meager	Average	Rich and well ordered	Rich, but chaotic	Chaotic

RELATION TO REALITY
(RORSCHACH, BELLEVUE-WECHSLER, DRAWINGS)

Fanatical exactitude	Not noticeably disturbed	Firm and good	"Artistic leeway"	Loose

USUAL — UNUSUAL THOUGHT CONTENT
(RORSCHACH, UNPLEASANT CONCEPT)

Stereotyped	Average	Original	Bizarre Qualities offset by other features	Bizarre

EMOTIONAL TONE (RORSCHACH, SZONDI)

Lacking, repressed	Struggling for expression	Warm, readily available	Getting out of hand	Emotions rampant

CONSTRUCTIVE FANTASY (RORSCHACH)

Absent	Average	Active	Active +	Topheavy, withdrawal

PASSIVITY — AGGRESSION
(RORSCHACH, SZONDI, UNPLEASANT CONCEPT)

Hampering passivity	Insufficient drive	Sufficient drive	Aggression +	Overpowering aggression

ested in is a personality appraisal, an independent evaluation of him as a person, prior to his intensive psychoanalytic work, which will be compared in a year, a year and a half, two years, with another, similar examination at the termination of treatment. The therapist in this instance is anxious for as much information about the patient as he can possibly obtain, since he is to work with him intensively for quite a long period of time. He is also interested in having the report from the tests available so that when the occasion arises and the time is right, he may perhaps discuss it directly with the patient. In these cases, I use various charts to plot a diagram or profile of the individual against which the second profile will be matched.

Physician: I certainly have a much clearer idea now of what it is you do with your time. You're really like a man with a mental X-ray machine to whom other physicians in the hospital refer their patients in order to corroborate or reinforce the diagnoses they have made by other means or, on occasion, to be surprised by new information.

Psychologist: Exactly. That mental X-ray analogy is, I think, the nearest we will come to describing our type of work.

Physician: All the time, however, you have spoken of the fact that patients have been referred to you by physicians. What would happen if a person just got a notion he wants to be examined and calls for an appointment?

Psychologist: As a matter of fact, this can be quite a problem. Occasionally one of the tests gets written up in some popular magazine, and I find that for a few weeks, I am inundated with telephone calls by persons who wish to be tested. These persons have to be refused, and many times they are annoyed at the refusal.

Physician: Well, I may be stupid, but I can't see why you can't accommodate them if they wish to come.

Psychologist: It's partly a matter of providing the best and most effective service. There probably would be no harm in telling an individual what he scored on one of the standard intelligence tests. I could also undoubtedly put him through various aptitude tests, allow him to take certain questionnaires in regard to his interests, and make a statement about him in terms of these qualities, which he could see without harm. But the tests which are used in psychodiagnosis may reveal very fundamental disturbances with which it would be quite impossible to acquaint the person directly, and without making provisions to help him handle the difficulties which had been revealed. Consequently, I would frequently be in possession of information about an individual which would be comparable to having taken a stomach X ray and discovered that he had cancer.

Again, I think your own analogy of the mental X ray will help you to see what I mean. No radiologist takes an X ray of the stomach without knowing where to refer the patient should the X ray prove to demonstrate severe pathology. My situation is exactly comparable when I examine someone I do not know, who has not been referred to me, and who has simply called the office on the telephone. If I find really serious psychological disturbance, what am I to do? I certainly cannot just announce this to the patient directly. On the other hand, I must somehow persuade him, without alarming him, that he needs professional help, and then the chances are that it will be up to me to spend many hours telephoning amongst my colleagues in an attempt to place him for therapy. This I personally consider as being the wrong way to go about. I admit that occasionally, in certain emergencies, it has to be done, but as a framework of operation, it is clearly unsatisfactory.

Physician: Would you go so far as to say you would never handle anything except through referral channels?

Psychologist: I would say that I prefer to handle them that way, but every now and again, something arises which begins and ends in this office. For instance, I have occasionally examined patients whose insight and maturity, whose general personality and intellectual integration were so outstanding, as demonstrated by the tests, that I have felt perfectly free to discuss with them some situational or immediate problem with the knowledge that such discussion would not precipitate any type of disastrous and excessive anxiety. However I find that referrals from schools, universities, physicians, clinics and other care-taking agencies usually result in more satisfactory service, since we can follow through with better planning for the person seeking help.

Physician: You know, I find all this quite intriguing, and I'm tempted to submit myself to your tests in order to experience them from the inside.

Psychologist: With that remark, you show your true scientific spirit. And you would make a good psychologist yourself.

Physician: How so?

Psychologist: From a long experience of dealing with students, some very genuinely interested in the subject, and some rather superficially, I have discovered that their attitude toward whether or not they wish to be tested themselves or merely study the results of other persons who have been tested, is a crucial, and, I might say, a diagnostic one. The person who is willing to look at himself from the inside is someone who may safely be trusted ultimately in looking at the insides of others. However, whether or not you wish, on further consideration, to be a real guinea pig, let me assure you that I would be delighted to have another discussion with you in order to go into some of the tests in more detail.

[II]

~~~~~~

Tools the Clinical Psychologist Uses

Physician: Well, here I am, all set for Lesson Two. You're going to tell me about the tests you use. First I want a bird's-eye view. Tell me what sort of information you're trying to get at. What are these projective techniques?

Psychologist: It's not easy in general terms to introduce you to the ideas which underlie all the projective methods. Or, let me put it another way, an introductory talk on the principles and theories underlying the projective testing should really be given at the end of a course of lectures in which you had concrete experience in all the projective techniques themselves. I know this sounds paradoxical, but it's actually the case. It's a dilemma in which I find myself again and again in teaching experience, for in order to make the introductory generalizations meaningful, the student should, ideally, be in possession of tangible and concrete information about the tests themselves. However, if I spend my time in my introduction giving such specific information about the various methods, we both become bogged down in detail, unable to see the woods for the trees.

Physician: I am willing to take some things for granted. I'll give you a lead. I have had experience, if you can call it that, with two tests. I once took an intelligence test — I answered a lot of questions and I had the feeling I got most of them right, so I must have come out with a pretty good score. Then one time in college, I took a questionnaire which asked me a lot of questions about myself. I was never very sure how well I'd done on that one. If I remember correctly, I tried to fix it up a little bit so as to look like the kind of student I thought the professor wanted to have!

Psychologist: That's a good starting point. I'll give you an analogy which may help you contrast the type of information extracted from a patient by way of the projective techniques as compared with the type of information derived from the tests you have mentioned, which I will call direct or objective techniques.

Let's suppose that I was testing your capacity to drive a car in two different ways. In terms of the direct or objective techniques, my instructions to you would be something like this: "Get in this particular car, drive around the block, park at this or that point. At the top of the hill make a turn, make such and such traffic signals, back the car into that roadway, and then drive back to me." The individual thus tested would pass or fail this examination in terms of whether he did or did not do what he was told to do on each of these specific items. I could score him as right or wrong, as having passed or failed, on any number of points that I liked to enumerate. Each of my candidates would be examined in the same way, and the information about each would be recorded uniformly.

By the same analogy, in terms of the projective techniques, I might say to my candidate for a driving license, just, "Show me how you drive." I would, therefore, leave the choice of the car up to him. Suppose he wished to take an old jalopy and, despite its antiquated years and erratic brakes, maneuver it strategically over a difficult road. This would be entirely up to him, and my appraisal of his driving would be in terms, not only of his performance, but of his choice of car, choice of route, and the type of things he wished to show me he could do. Another candidate might wish to display extremely fast driving in his racer. He might even suggest that I come to a dirt track to see him racing. A third might elect to maneuver in and out of New York on a highway during a rush hour. The differences between the two types of examination are, therefore, the extent to which the burden of proof is placed on the individual to show his capacities and achievements.

In evaluating my three candidates in the second type of testing, which is analogous to the projective techniques, I would do so in terms of their total pattern of performance. I would not score them point for point on any uniform scale, as I could with a series of candidates operating under a more restricted and uniform set of instructions.

Physician: Well, it looks to me as if what you're saying is that in the projective techniques there really are no answers, or no types of performance which can be considered right or wrong in and of themselves. Anything may be appropriate or inappropriate, depending on the total setting.

Psychologist: That's an excellent point. Why don't you develop it a little further?

Physician: Well, what I was thinking of, for example, was that going 'round a bend at forty miles an hour is not anything out of the ordinary if you're driving a good solid automobile. But going around the same bend of the road in an old jalopy with its inadequate brakes and perhaps a horn that didn't work, at that same speed, would be just plain foolishness. One and the same speed, that is, can be perfectly appropriate or it may be a daredevil stunt.

Psychologist: Supposing I pushed you and forced you to say whether going around a bend at forty miles an hour was right or wrong.

Physician: Well, I wouldn't quite know how to answer. I don't know how it can be answered yes or no; it's within the speed limits in most states, I suppose, but that doesn't take into account the fellow whose equipment is not equal to it. I see what you mean: you don't have to prove your point anymore. What you're telling me is that in the objective type of testing an answer can *only* be right or wrong. There are no other possibilities. In the intelligence test I took, for example, I either knew or didn't know a specific piece of information. But you've got some sort of tests which allow the fellow more leeway to express himself; at the same time, you've come up with the idea that some of the things he expresses about himself may be good or bad, right or wrong *for him*, depending on other factors.

Psychologist (reaching for a book): Well, now let me try out a definition on you to see if it makes sense. Here is one given by Lawrence Frank in his book, *Projective Methods*. "The projective methods are designed to permit a study of the unique, idiomatic individual which is conceived as a process of organizing experience and so must elude the investigator who relies on methods that of necessity ignore the configurational quality of each personality."

Physician: Hey, wait a moment. That's getting much too abstract for me. I don't understand your psychological terminology. Take me back to your good old concrete analogies.

Psychologist: It's really not so difficult as it appears. What it is saying is that the direct way of testing the individual, even of testing his driving a car, if we stick to the old analogy, misses the essential aspects of that individual, since that is given by the total patterning of his performance and that patterning is the "unique" way of operating for him. Perhaps I can put it in another way. The projective methods provide the opportunity for the individual to *project outside* of himself a pattern or organization of stresses and strains which are *within him*. And by the organization given to the visible and concrete test material, he allows the examiner to understand his hidden dynamics.

Physician: There we go again. "Project outside of himself . . . strains and stresses within him . . . organization of visible test material . . . hidden dynamics. . . ." You're going to have to do some more explanation.

Psychologist: Well, let's take them one by one. What do you think of in connection with the word "projection?"

Physician: Of a projection lantern.

Psychologist: That'll do very nicely. What happens in the case of the projection lantern is that a slide which is *inside* the lantern gets *projected* onto a screen in such a way that all of us sitting in an auditorium can see what is on one slide even though, of course, we cannot see the slide itself. Now there is something else of importance. The screen on which the slide is projected must be a plain, homogeneous, uniform surface, so that whatever is projected on it is the only thing that we see. What do you suppose would happen if the slide were projected on a picture that was hanging on the wall?

Physician: Why, there'd be complete confusion between what was on the slide and what was on the picture. You wouldn't be able to tell what was what.

Psychologist: Exactly. So in the projective techniques we have to use the kind of test material which is as "blank" and as meaningless as possible, so that we know that anything that appears on it results from what was "projected onto it."

As a matter of fact, that which is described as "projection" is not something new or mysterious at all, nor does it result from a specialized way of approaching things. We all project ourselves all day long and are always looking at the projections of others. The only way, for example, that we know that one person is a "tidy" person and the other is an "untidy" person is by looking at the state of affairs of the rooms in which, let us say, they change their clothes. The room, in this instance, is the "projective material" onto which X's tidy behavior and Y's untidy behavior are projected. We make our deductions about X and Y in terms of the organization of the objects (the scattered or the tidily arranged clothes) which they leave behind them. These clothes have been so "patterned" by the "organizing properties" belonging to X and Y, respectively. The various tests spoken of as the projective methods are merely controlled, repeatable, comparatively simple situations on which individuals can leave their imprint and their particular way of arranging, patterning, or organizing their experiences and actions.

Physician: Your use of the word "imprint" gives me an idea. Let me see if I understand what you're talking about by giving you an example. I'm walking along the beach and I see ahead of me two sets of footprints in the sand. Like this:

Even though I don't see a person and a dog, I know that they've been walking there for each has "organized" that blank bit of sand according to his own pattern. How's that?

Psychologist: That's an excellent example. In this case, of course, the imprint left by the person and the dog relates to the physical characteristics of their feet. In the projective techniques, we are picking up characteristics of mental and emotional reactions. But you are quite right in that you *deduce* a person and a dog which are nowhere to be seen, from the way they respectively "organize" the sand.

Now, what were some of the other phrases which you objected to?

Physician: How about "strains and stresses," and "hidden dynamics?"

Psychologist: All right. Let me take another type of analogy. Imagine some big physical plant which generates power of various kinds. In the control room of such a hypothetical place there would be a number of dials indicating various pressures in various parts of this complicated physical system. Looking at the physical plant from the outside, however, it would be quite impossible to get the type of information on its "hidden dynamics" that you could get from reading the dials in the control room.

On such dials you might see, for instance, that too much pressure was building up in one part of the system at a given time and this would have to be diverted or discharged in some way or a disastrous explosion might take place.

Information derived from the projective techniques may, I think, be justly likened to this, for here we are sometimes able to see these hidden dynamics, strains and stresses on our projective instruments which are comparable to the dials which record the pressure in the physical plant. If one looks at an individual in a casual fashion, even if one examines him in a face to face interview, it may not be possible to get the information about the *relative strength* of the various strains and stresses. From the projective techniques we are able to gauge to what extent the individual's psychological energy has been diverted into any one psychological system to the exclusion of or at the expense of others. There are ways of appraising to what extent a given disturbance permeates the system at large or is relatively well localized.

Physician: Some of your tests, then, are able to predict whether an individual is about to explode psychologically and in which of various ways he may be expected to blow his top! And then you have others which enable people to leave their psychological footprints on the sand so that, studying these footprints, you get the patterns of their mental makeup.

Psychologist: Exactly. And you have provided yourself with two good working analogies for the basic ideas underlying the projectives. As you come to understand each of the tests in greater detail, perhaps as you come to take them yourself, you will see how your analogies fit.

[III]

~~~~~~

Some Unnecessary
Misunderstandings

Physician: I'm glad you could come over this evening, Smith. I began to feel guilty about dropping into your office so often during your working hours. The fact is, the more I think about this work you're doing, the more questions come to my mind. I am really catching on to what these projective tests of yours may mean. You know, I've just realized that I am interpreting the "projections" of others all the time, to say nothing of projecting myself in some way or another in everything I do. What a good thing there aren't too many psychologists around or life might become quite uncomfortable!

Let's see. I have jotted down several things I wanted to ask you. First of all, is there such a thing as a really normal human being? Or, let me put it this way, what constitutes "within normal limits" in your test findings?

Then I wanted to know to what extent you are influenced by the patient as you see him. Aren't you likely to pick up some ideas about him even in speaking to him, watching him handle the tests, and so on? Are your findings influenced by this more than you think?

I also found myself bothered by the fact that so much seems to depend on so little. Here you go making pronouncements about brain tumors or the degree of an individual's anxiety, about which of the partners is the seriously disturbed individual in the marital problem, and all this is derived from a couple of tests. And I'm not finished yet. I want to know, do you all come up with the same answer once you have given the tests? If I refer the patient to you and then to one of your psychological colleagues, would I get the same information from both of you? And, finally, could you all be wrong on a case, even though you all came up with the same answer?

Psychologist: Let me start with the idea of "within normal limits" — a very useful idea and one that is likely to be overlooked by some psychologists who emphasize almost exclusively the deviations in their findings. But the problem of "normality" is a tough one. It is a word we use in two distinct ways and often skip back and forth between the two meanings without realizing it. In the first place, there is the use of the word "normal" in the sense of average or statistically frequent. In the second, it is used in the sense of optimal functioning or absence of abnormality. For example, in the first sense, it is perfectly normal to have a cold. Almost every individual has had one. There is nothing unusual or abnormal about it, speaking in the first sense. Speaking in the second sense, however, the body is not functioning in its optimal or normal condition when the individual has a cold. Or, again, no one considers it in any way abnormal if we are not experts in our chosen field of sports. Most people who play games for recreation or amusement play quite abnormally as far as the game itself is concerned, yet it is normal statistically to play poorly or abnormally. You can probably think of other medical examples.

Physician: Sure. It is perfectly normal for the kidney to have dead glomeruli, but in and of itself, a dead glomerulus is not normal. And it is perfectly normal in the first sense which you spoke of to have a cavity in the tooth filled, but a tooth with a cavity is not a normal tooth as far as its internal well-being is concerned.

Psychologist: Exactly. And you can see where I'm heading. First, if one thinks of normal in the sense of "statistically most frequent" it is perfectly normal to have an abnormal or inadequate personality reflected in the test findings! I might put it another way. I suppose I have available now some five or six thousand test records. These have been obtained from persons of all walks of life, and by no means have all of them been referred on account of personality problems. As a matter of fact, many of them were doing extremely well and functioning very adequately at the time they were tested. And yet I suppose only four or five individuals out of that large sample have fulfilled the potentialities claimed for the normal or optimal personality as reflected by these particular test instruments. It has to be stated, therefore, that the vast majority of the so-called normally behaving individuals, individuals, that is, who are symptom-free as far as their doctor or psychiatrist is concerned, individuals who are holding a job and are satisfactorily embedded in family life, these individuals as far as the test findings go still fall short of the optimal achievement which the tests prescribe.

Physician: I want to come back to some other aspects of this later, but tell me now what does the hypothetical paragon look like in your tests? The very small percentage of people who have seemed to fulfill themselves satisfactorily, how are they described in terms of your frame of reference?

Psychologist: This hypothetical paragon, as you so justly call him, is an individual with an inexhaustible store of personal resources, interests, and, for what the term is worth, rich, inner experience. He has a ballast of satisfying thoughts, intriguing and constructive fantasy, and mental initiative which stands him in good stead so that virtually none of the slings and arrows of outrageous fortune throw him out of his own equanimity. On the other hand, this highly intriguing and enticing personal life has not so caught him in its clutches that he is unwilling to be attentive to the demands of the world around him. He is able to relinquish the hold it has on him when other demands require his being absorbed outside himself.

Secondly, this hypothetical paragon would have sufficient drive to externalize and make concrete, that is, to put to practical action, his constructive fantasies. This drive must also lead him to a positive solution of his psycho-sexual needs. It must enable him to take an aggressive stand when the occasion demands, but he must not be so overpoweringly aggressive that it is impossible for him to assume a more passive or receptive role in a relationship. He should be able to speak but also to listen, to pursue his own aims aggressively but not relentlessly, to be dominant but not domineering.

This individual should be relatively free from anxiety, and here, of course, is one of the points where we must underline *hypothetical*. It is, in actuality, probably unthinkable that an individual go through life without an anxious moment. However, our paragon must have no psychosomatic symptoms or concern over bodily functions. He must, of course, be free from phobias and from the more general manifestations of vague anxiety.

Then he must be an individual of good self-control. He must always be able to do what he sets out to do and must not be at the mercy of outbursts of emotion or moods of depression. On the other hand, steering between Scylla and Charybdis, he must not develop this control to too great an extent or he would stifle spontaneity within himself and would tend toward a rigidity not sanctioned by the prescribed norms of the test.

Our hypothetical individual must also be sensitive and understanding of other persons, but not so sensitive that he is thrown off guard by unimportant details and loses perspective of the total situation. He must be someone able to enjoy fully the experiences of the senses, but never, let us say, to the point where he is bogged down and merely receptive without concomitant action. Our hypothetical individual would, then, enjoy music and artistic creations to the fullest, but he would not be unable to renounce these pleasures if they interfered with other things. Most important, he would have a virtually inexhaustible store of warmth, feeling and love for other human beings. This would be readily available and would not be blocked or cause him anxiety in its expression. Its central core would be satisfactorily anchored to some individual of his choice. And, more important even than these essential personality ingredients, all of which can be measured by the projective techniques, would be the relationship which they bear, one to another. The tests prescribe that there are certain maximum or optimal ratios in the sense that certain of these qualities are entitled to a larger expenditure of the individual's psychological bank balance than others. And what makes normality in the sense of optimal functioning so rare is that it is unusual to find these particular proportions correct in all instances.

Physician: As you spoke, I couldn't help thinking of the chart you demonstrated the other day and which you said would become more meaningful as I got to know something more about the tests. It seems to me that, in describing your hypothetical normal, you are describing an individual who would appear in a certain position on your chart. (*See* pages 9, 16, 18.) For example, you mentioned that his fantasy must be active and satisfying, but not such as to lead him to withdraw into it. He should have sufficient drive but not an overpowering one and his emotions should be warm and readily available. I imagine that other things you mentioned could be epitomized equally well on your chart.

Psychologist: That is perfectly correct. The central column of the five, with the exception of that which deals with straight intelligence, is meant to portray the happy medium, the balance between too much and too little of the various component psychological ingredients which we are discussing. That practically no one falls exclusively within the central column is another way of demonstrating the fact that completely optimal functioning is hardly ever found.

Physician: Now do a job of convincing me that, unlike the fortune-teller who is really assessing his client while pretending to gaze into the crystal ball, you actually base your information on what the tests give you and not what you unconsciously assimilate from the many clues which the patient is giving you in his behavior.

Psychologist: I think the best answer to that is simply to state the fact that the psychologist who will do the interpretation of the test does not *need* to see the patient at all; that is, he can work on the test findings which have been taken for him by a colleague or a competent assistant. And I should also add that when he does examine the patient himself, he should make a careful distinction between his clinical impressions, on the one hand, recording these faithfully, and the test findings, on the other. I have made it routine practice in the reports which I turn in to begin with a description of how the patient acted. I also record it on the chart you saw, under the MANNER DURING TESTS. It is interesting to point up the discrepancies between the clinical impression and the test findings. For example, some individuals have a beautiful "front." Their facade gives no indication of the extent and depth of the turmoil inside. It is a very strange feeling to record material which, from experience, one knows to be indicative of very serious psychopathology, while, at the same time, one sits side by side with an individual who appears perfectly composed, rational, and perhaps slightly supercilious of the whole test proceedings.

Conversely, some of the individuals who appear during the test interview to be overwrought and extremely anxious give indications of excellent personality integration and a great richness of resources despite superficial turmoil. Provided the psychologist keeps these two types of indications separate, it seems wise for him to do his own testing except in special cases.

This leads us, however, to another question you did not bring up but which is an important one, namely, should the psychologist be supplied with relevant medical or psychiatric findings at the time he is asked to see the patient, or should he work "blind"?

Some years ago, when the projective techniques were new, not widely known, and still a somewhat controversial issue, a great many psychologists resorted to the practice of making only "blind" analyses. This meant that they would be sent patients without any comments from the referring doctor so that their reports, based on the test findings alone, could not in any way have been influenced by the existing clinical impression.

Physician: Well, that seems fair enough to me. If you have to make your report in terms of the test findings only, why do you need to know anything about the patient from the physician's angle?

Psychologist: There are clearly two schools of thought involved, and if a *completely independent evaluation* of the patient is wanted, it is perfectly justifiable to ask the psychologist to do it "blind." However, in my opinion, more satisfactory results are obtained if the psychologist knows something about the problem that faces the physician. As a matter of fact, it is not common medical practice to keep colleagues in the dark. If you refer a patient for X ray, you specify that the plates should be taken of the lungs or the skull or the leg which might be fractured. You do not ask that the radiologist waste his time X-raying all additional parts of the body in order to come up with unbiased findings in regard to the chest plates. It does not in any way invalidate the electrocardiographic findings that by virtue of the fact that the patient was sent for such examination some heart lesion is suspected. Again, the electroencephalographic recordings are just as objective if the patient is referred to that department with a statement that a tumor is suspected in the left frontal lobe. Nor would you accuse the technician of being influenced one way or the other if he is asked to look for tubercle bacilli on a slide taken from the patient's sputum. The problem becomes different for the psychologist only because the physician is completely unaware of the raw material or what the test records (on which the psychologist bases his report) look like.

Physician: I think you have put your finger on the difficulty right there. Although I am not a radiologist and do not consider myself a specialist in that field, I can nonetheless discuss the plates with our X-ray man. If I disagree with his findings, I can say so, basing my case on the films we are both looking at. But I am unaware of what it is that enables you to draw your conclusions, and if I don't want to accept your pronouncements as correct as a matter of course, I suppose I would want to make the situation as watertight as possible and I would demand that you prove to me that you've got something.

Psychologist: It is not that I don't understand your desire to take precautions. The trouble is that if every physician continues to have to prove things for himself, the most beneficial type of collaboration will be a long time coming. It is my hope that in these discussions with you, you will persevere long enough to see something of the actual raw material of the tests that are used in common practice.

Let me give you one or two brief examples of how much information is wasted if the specific problem is not known to the psychologist. I will reverse the case of the young medical student I discussed with you at our first meeting. This time we will assume that the psychiatrist who referred the case suspected a brain tumor but that, on the other hand, the psychological test findings gave no indication of this whatsoever. Suppose, however, that the psychiatrist does not mention his suspicion when he refers the patient. Since the possibility of a tumor is so rare, it might never occur to the psychologist in his report to make a specific statement *ruling out* its presence. But if the psychologist knows that a tumor is suspected, then in his report he can rule out quite specifically the presence of an organic lesion by demonstrating his evidence in favor of his negative finding. If the psychiatrist expects an answer to a specific question, *but does not give the question*, then the chances are that the personality appraisal and evaluation may seem to him vague and irrelevant. It is true, they *will* be vague and irrelevant *with reference to that specific but unformulated question*. On the other hand, if the question has been formulated, the whole test procedure can be oriented relevantly to the proving or disproving of this particular hypothesis.

Physician: That puts the matter in a somewhat different light. I expect from what you say that you are sometimes criticized because you are not a mind reader!

Psychologist: I have sometimes felt that, but, seriously, it's impossible to be as helpful as we might be if we only have to guess at the reasons for the referral. Let me give you one more example which may show you more clearly why reports sometimes misfire through lack of adequate information. Take the case referred by a physician whose usual, almost routine, question has been the request that the tests rule out the possibility of an underlying or latent schizophrenia. But on a given occasion, he refers a patient whose problem relates only to his antagonism to his father and, in this instance, he wishes to come to a decision as to whether or not it would be wise to send the boy away from home. The psychologist, unaware of this specific problem, bends his efforts and time in his report to the ruling out of the presence of an underlying schizophrenic process. This, it so happens, is of no interest to the psychiatrist in this particular case.

Physician: But if the psychologist had known the actual problem, would not that have in some way influenced him?

Psychologist: In what way could he have been influenced? The purpose of the test is not one of demonstrating whether or not the psychologist can arrive, without outside information, at the same *problem* which confronts the psychiatrist! The purpose of the test is to adduce information from other sources, about aspects of the patient's personality which may not be accessible in a clinical interview. If, in this instance, the psychologist knows the problem, namely that there is a question as to whether or not this particular boy should be sent away from home, he can assess his strengths and weaknesses with a view to making some evaluation of his capacities for launching out on an independent career.

Physician: But supposing I am genuinely baffled by a patient and do not know how to pigeonhole him psychiatrically, nor even have the "feel" of him as a person, can I not refer him to see what you fellows make of him?

Psychologist: Fair enough. But in this instance, you would have given your psychological colleague all the information that he needs, namely, that he is to go ahead with a general, overall appraisal and he is not expected to come up with the answer to some particular problem that has never even been formulated for him. For every case that is referred there must not be a specific problem, but *when* such a problem exists, it can only be answered relevantly if it has been formulated to begin with.

Let's go on now to the other question you raised as to the extent of agreement between psychological colleagues as to diagnosis of the individual's stresses and strains. Let me turn the question around and ask you honestly how many specialists in your field are one hundred per cent correct and how often do all of your colleagues always agree with you?

Physician: I would say off the bat that anyone in medicine claiming he had a test that was one hundred per cent correct was either very inexperienced or a liar. I'd say the same about anyone who had never had a difference of opinion about a diagnosis. For instance, in their early stages, influenza can be confused with virus pneumonia, chicken pox with smallpox, brain tumor or platybasia with multiple sclerosis.

Psychologist: How about the Wassermann Test? Would you say that if it were positive, beyond any possible doubt the individual had syphilis?

Physician: As I told you, no test is a hundred per cent certain. There can be false positives in any of them. A Wassermann may be correct in ninety per cent of the cases, but there may be ten per cent which may ultimately prove to have been erroneous. Malaria, high fever, mononucleosis can give false positives.

Psychologist: I think that is all the information I need from you in order to answer your question and to show you that, by and large, psychological tests have the same margin of error as do those concerned with somatic phenomena. There is first the factor of inexperience. There will be psychologists who, in the course of their careers, will have to learn the hard way, namely, by making mistakes. Some of the complex factors will be overlooked or the psychologist's judgment will not be based on enough actual cases so that his decisions will have been guided by textbook abstractions. He may fail to give sufficient weight to some of the psychological ingredients and may have been too much impressed by others, just as, in your field, a young intern's judgment may be swung by giving too much emphasis to some of the symptoms and overlooking others.

Then there will be the question of differences of opinion which arise from the different backgrounds of the conflicting specialists. For example, the psychologist who has been trained primarily on the psychiatric wards may be almost too sensitive to indices of psychosis and will tend to find them in other samples of the population, and, while it is true that he will be reacting to characteristic responses in the tests which were undoubtedly found amongst his psychotic patients, he may not have had sufficient experience with a large enough cross-section of adequately functioning individuals to realize that these same traits may be absorbed successfully if they are offset by others.

Physician: Then I should not expect necessarily to get a final, conclusive, and irrevocable answer from you on a difficult diagnostic problem?

Psychologist: By no means. Any psychologist who sets himself up as having information of a different order of reliability from that of his medical or psychiatric colleagues is fooling himself as well as them. As a matter of fact, I might read you something that was written on this point some years ago. The writer was attempting to define the characteristics that entitled the psychologist to call himself a "*clinical* psychologist," when our profession was still in its infancy:

"The psychologist is entitled to the epithet 'clinical' when he ceases to consider himself as the infallible psycho-diagnostician — God's gift to the psychiatrist! Or, on the other hand, when he is past the stage of thinking of himself as 'successful' only in terms of the number of the times when his diagnoses equate with those of the psychiatrist, being elated when his batting average rises, plunged into the depths of despair as his 'diagnoses' differ.

"Unpopular though this suggestion may be, I personally would like to see even the word 'psychodiagnostician' dispensed with, in that it is somewhat pretentious and inaccurate! Actually, psychiatrists do not need the services of psychologists, clinical or otherwise, to make a diagnosis, except in a very few cases. While it may be spectacular, for instance, to call attention to the presence of organic cerebral pathology when none has been suspected, and to have it verified by X ray, while it may be satisfying to validate 'objectively' the psychiatrist's opinion of an underlying schizophrenic process in the demonstrable deviations which appear in the pliable materials of the projective techniques, such cases, though gratifying, form a very small percentage of those a psychiatrist sees or refers.

"I would prefer, therefore, for the Clinical Psychologist to emerge in a more positive role, in that of what I might call the assessor, surveyor, or map maker of the dimensions and depths of personality, or to see him envisaged as an explorer of the individual's potentialities and resources. Thus his task would not lie in the diagnosis of a neurosis, but rather in a description of the type of personality in which the neurotic symptoms were finding expression. For when all is said and done, diagnosis is a small part of the battle for all concerned. The psychological clinician must realize that his information is valid in its own right, and that it needs to be presented in such a manner that the therapist can best make use of it in planning for the patient's welfare. He must remember that his long suit lies in being able to answer the question 'What personality resources does this patient possess?' developing, if necessary, new categories, new patterns of personality, new clinical entities, if his material so demonstrates.

"Because of our inevitable lack of orientation in the medical and psychiatric fields, we, as psychologists, are only just reaching the point where we can refrain from the attempt to fit our findings into the pre-existing pigeonholes, where we are realizing that our task lies in presenting our material in a way that does least damage to it.

"In the same way, the psychological clinician, in his role of explorer or surveyor, must have reached a point of belief in his own materials and his own capacities so that he is unabashed to report negative findings, where necessary; and he is willing to report his failure to detect clinically suspected trends without feelings of guilt and insecurity. He must realize that his recording cameras, so to speak, are often set at different angles from those of the psychiatrist, and therefore that his picture of the person under scrutiny may look different, and that often the very discrepancy between the two pictures may be important in assessing the total personality."*

* From *Training in Clinical Psychology*. Transactions of the First Conference March 27-28, 1947, New York City. Publication of Josiah Macy, Jr. Foundation, New York City.

Physician: The only trouble with getting involved in this sort of discussion is that I no sooner get one question cleared up than I begin to think of others. I don't know where I got the idea, but I had the feeling that some psychologists specialized in the use of only one test, making their diagnoses and reports in terms of its findings alone, whereas you seem to imply that you can utilize a series of tests interchangeably and that when you examine a patient, you subject him to quite a few.

Psychologist: I think it is safe and fair to say that at the present time the majority of psychologists feel that a battery or a series of tests is a more effective type of examination than the concentration on any one instrument to the exclusion of all others. However, it should be said in fairness to those who base their findings on a single test that the extent, or the amount of experience which the psychologist has had with it, perhaps over a period of 15 or 20 years, enables him to extract from a single instrument a great deal of material. You are probably referring to the Rorschach Test, which was the earliest projective technique and which is still frequently used without benefits derived from other testing procedures.

Physician: Yes, now that you speak of it, I have heard people refer to "Rorschachs," but I have never known what it meant.

Psychologist: It is my intention to subject you to this particular test at our next meeting! But with reference to what you say, most psychologists now feel that the Rorschach can and should be amplified by a test that measures intelligence, as, for example, the well-known Wechsler-Bellevue, and by several other instruments which we may

go into later in detail. One of the main reasons *why* a battery of tests is valuable is that some individuals' performances on the battery itself vary so greatly, whereas other
individuals show considerable uniformity. Regardless of
how good any one instrument is, it is impossible to pick
up discrepancies between it and other tests, when using it
alone. To my mind these inter-test discrepancies are often
very revealing.

Physician: But if you give so many tests, isn't this an exhausting procedure for your patient? Doesn't he lose interest
or become fatigued?

Psychologist: How many tests a patient should be subjected to is not something that can be answered categorically.
Naturally he must not be overtaxed and the psychologist
must know where to break the testing procedure if signs of
fatigue are apparent. But there is also the question of how
valuable the sheer amassing of information about any given
individual can be. The more tests that are given, the more
material there will be to work over and the more the psychologist will be tied up with a proper evaluation of that
particular case. One might almost say that testing can become, for the perfectionist, such a work of art that there is
almost no limit to the amount of time he needs to think
about his material and extract from it every last drop of
information about his patient. But there comes a point where
the law of diminishing returns sets in and whereas the psychologist in his role of an "artist" may feel inclined to spend
many hours in the luxury of contemplating his findings, in
his role of a professional person with a series of jobs to be
done in a given time, he must often curtail and limit himself
in regard to any given case. In subjecting the patient to a

battery of tests, it is probably fair to say that no one test can be handled as exhaustively as it would have been were it the only instrument used.

Physician: I think I've come to the point where I should like to experience, rather than talk about, the tests. Do you have a free hour tomorrow?

Psychologist: Drop over in the late afternoon and we'll tackle one of them then.

PART TWO

The Creation of Miniature Psychological Worlds

Physician: Here I am, all set to be a guinea pig. I'm amused at myself. Your statement the other day that the best psychologists wanted to experience the tests from inside rather than merely observing the reactions of others in them must have had the desired effect! What are we to begin with?

Psychologist: I thought we'd start with the Rorschach Test. It's probably the most widely used and generally known of the projective techniques. It's forty years now since Hermann Rorschach, a Swiss psychiatrist, published his first description of it in Switzerland, and since then it has become almost a household word in medical and psychological circles and even amongst the public at large.

Physician: Sure thing. I saw pictures of those inkblots in *Time* Magazine some years ago; and my wife and I were at a movie the other night where the heroine's fate hung on the results of a Rorschach Test. But I still don't know anything about it so you'd better begin at the beginning. What do I do?

Psychologist: Your task in taking the test is to look at ten inkblot pictures which I shall present to you one after the other, and describe to me, as accurately as you can, what you see in them or in any part of them. That is the Rorschach Test, or perhaps I should say that is the basic technique for any inkblot test, whether you are looking at the ten original inkblots devised by Rorschach, or at any of the subsequently constructed series of which there are several. In the meantime, I will be taking down verbatim what you say. When you have finished, I shall want to be sure that I know exactly which parts of the blots you were looking at as you gave me your answers, and I may then go on to ask you a few more questions in order to elicit as much information as possible about what you saw.

Physician: Is that all there is to it? But how is it possible to tell so much about a person from such an insignificant procedure?

Psychologist: That's one of the questions I'll have to answer in some detail before you will be satisfied that you have really understood the test. As a matter of fact, it's one of the most frequent and legitimate expressions of skepticism that any thinking person voices. Sooner or later, somebody says about all psychological tests, "How can you draw such far-reaching conclusions from such slight clues?" But it is always easy to think that the clues from another fellow's discipline or body of knowledge are slight when we do not understand the background of information against which these clues are seen. For example, I think you will agree that such a "slight clue" as scratching the sole of the patient's foot to elicit a Babinski response *in and of itself* hardly seems to justify the kind of conclusions which can be drawn from it in regard to the lesions in the pyramidal tract. To the medically uninitiated, the movement of a big toe is really no more dignified or impressive in itself than the response to a blot of ink!

Physician: I think you psychologists are in an unusually vulnerable spot in this matter because, basically, no one likes to think that so much can be revealed about their psychological lives. I am just thinking of my own reaction in other specialties. I'm impressed when my geologist friend picks up a stone on the beach and makes a pronouncement about the age of the earth from it. I am also staggered when an archaeologist shows me a small fragment of pottery and then is able to recognize and reconstruct from it a thirteenth century B.C. vase. But I find myself experiencing a kind of resentment when you draw conclusions about emotional stability and personality organization — a word I have now learned to use — from what I might see in an inkblot. The very idea that it is so easy to be assessed psychologically is somehow distressing. One becomes vulnerable to the extent that the apparently trivial has meaning and significance.

Psychologist: You have put your finger on something extremely important in regard to some people's attitudes about psychological investigations. One is almost forced, at times, to ridicule psychological procedures because to accept the significance of the apparently trivial is to lay oneself open to psychological assessment.

Physician: I have another difficulty right here and that's in relation to the fact that after all there are only ten inkblots and this investigation, once we get started, is not going to last more than an hour. How do I know that *this hour* is typical for me in my life? Mightn't I do quite differently tomorrow or the next day?

Psychologist: Yes and no. There may be, from day to day, slight variations. But the chances are that the main characteristics of your performance today would hold good tomorrow or next week or next month provided nothing of epoch-making psychological importance intervened. This objection that you have just raised is not as serious as you might think. For example, in order to make an accurate blood count, how much blood would you need to take?

Physician: Why, just enough for a smear on a slide — hardly any.

Psychologist: Well, you see, that's a very, very small percentage of the blood in a patient's body. But this small sample is sufficient because it is *representative* of the total. If *it* contains too many white cells then it is a perfectly reasonable assurance that this imbalance will pertain throughout the whole bloodstream.

Or let us take an example in terms of time. A basal metabolic rate, although determined during a period of only a few minutes, can be extrapolated so that it is indicative of the rate of energy metabolism of the patient throughout the day under the same conditions.

So, to return to the investigation of an individual in a psychological test-situation, we are *sampling* the way he perceives and organizes the meaningless, and this will be representative of his perception outside the testing situation. If what I will call the "perceptual ingredients" show a balance or imbalance in the small test-tube sample of the inkblot, we may assume that the balance or imbalance will hold for the way he looks at the world at large.

Physician: Although I don't know yet what you mean by a balance or imbalance of perceptual ingredients, I think your arguments about sampling in general answer my questions or my apprehensions that I will not do myself justice in the small space of time allotted to me! If it won't upset the testing procedure, however, and if you're in the mood for it, I should like to ask you one or two more things before we begin.

Psychologist: By all means. It is more important that you get a feel and understanding of the test than that you submit to it in a routine or professionally naive fashion. In fact, I am going to feel free to stop you at any time and discuss your answers with you in order to make the *test itself* understandable, something I would never do with a patient, or with anyone for whom the prime purpose of the testing was for the examiner to acquire valid material.

Physician: I think all I am trying to say is: Why do you have to have *inkblots?* Or tell me again the significance of why we are using meaningless material. When we were talking the other day, in describing the projective techniques in general, you made quite a point about the test material being of such a kind that the individual being tested could impose upon it his own pattern of mental activity thereby recording his own "idiomatic" ways of working. Can you tell me a little more about this?

Psychologist: Let me approach it from a different angle. It has long been accepted in animal psychology that in order to see how an animal behaved, how intelligent it was, or how quickly it could learn, the unsuspecting beast was placed in a new and *meaningless situation* and allowed to sink, swim, or grapple with the unforeseen as best it might. In this case, the all-knowing experimenter immersed it, so to speak, in a meaningless world and sat back to watch the results.

Physician: But isn't it more difficult to throw human beings into situations which are really new to them? I have always liked that line of the poet Bridges* in which he says, "And wisdom lies in masterful administration of the unforeseen," but I would think that the experimental and controlled production of the bonafide "unforeseen" must be hard to achieve.

Psychologist: It is very difficult. As a matter of fact, in order to be immersed in a meaningless world, a really new total environment, we would have to be transplanted, let us say, to Mars, or to have hypothetical men from Mars, people who had entirely different sets of meanings, come here and construct the experimental situation into which we would then be put. But, since we cannot do this, the best we can achieve is to try to find an experimental environment which is as neutral, new, and devoid of known signals as possible.

Now, insofar as you look fixedly at the picture that I will now give you, you are, for the time being, immersed in a new and meaningless environment. In other words, looking at the picture before you, you are in a new world. What are the properties of this "world"? What do you see in it?

Physician: I see two men facing each other and holding out their hands, warming them, I think, over a large red brazier of glowing coals.† Behind are two bright lights. The

* Bridges, Robert: *The Testament of Beauty*, p. 1.
† This inkblot (Fig. I) originally appeared in two colors with the center and uppermost blots in red.—Ed.

Fig. I

Fig. II

men are friendly and engaged in animated conversation on a topic that is of interest to both of them. As a matter of fact, they may even be physicians who've been out skiing, for it seems as though they have snow on their clothes and a little bit on their hair. That would also account for their huge boots, though I don't know what the spikes are on the ends of them.

Psychologist: There is a great deal in this one answer you have given which can be used as a basis for understanding the test as a whole. Before I do this, however, let me give you some other responses to this same picture, some other miniature psychological worlds created out of meaninglessness.

An eleven-year-old boy whom I tested the other day commented, "This is the picture of a boy who has just taken something that he wants away from another one." His twin brother, tested an hour or so later, looking at the same picture, remarked, " This is the picture of a boy who has just had his things taken away from him."

Physician: It is not difficult to see which of the boys is the aggressive and dominant twin!

Psychologist: You are quite right, and here you find yourself making a rather significant comment on the basis of a very slight clue! But as you have correctly surmised, looking at the meaningless inkblots, each of the twins has constructed part of a world along the lines on which he is wont to experience and organize things in his everyday life.

So, in understanding a patient's Rorschach record, we have to let him speak to us in this way. We have to realize that no created gesture, no created person or thing is arbitrary. That which is seen and the way in which it is seen reflects properties the individual has experienced as characteristic of the world around him.

Starting with these examples, let us consider three ways of evaluating them. First, *what* was seen? In this instance, "two men" by you, "two boys" by the twins. In other words, *human beings* were seen by by all of you.

Then, *how* were they seen? For you, they were "talking and warming their hands over a brazier" and had "come in from skiing." In the case of the twins, one was seen as if *accepting passively* an action that had been done to him, while the other was seen as engaged in the *aggressive act* of taking something away.

Then, how "good" was that which was seen, and by "good" I mean, how realistic, how sensible, or how justified, in terms of the gross shape of the inkblot, is each of these answers?*

Let us deal first with this question of the justification or the extent to which an answer is "good," legitimate, and sensible as opposed to being unjustified, bizarre, or without reference to reality. It would be agreed on by most people that there is nothing outrageous in considering that part of the inkblot as representing a man or a boy, although it is true that neither men nor boys have proportionately such large feet, nor spike protuberances at the ends of them. (It is interesting in this connection that you were more bothered by the spike protuberances than were the boys, who completely ignored or disregarded them.) In contrast to such "legitimate" answers, to call these same parts of the blot the "letter M," a "piano," a "rhinoceros," a "submarine," a "table," a "horse," a "bookshelf," could not be considered justified by the objective shape.

* cf. Chapter I, p. 10.

So, one of the characteristics of paramount importance in estimating a type of psychological world which the individual is constructing from the meaningless materials is whether or not, within reasonable limits, it conforms to reality.

Let us turn back again to *what* was seen. Of the many human forms which might have been chosen with approximately equal justification, those selected by the twins are boys of approximately their own age. You amplified your first response of "men" so that your human figures were *"doctors who had been skiing."* In both instances, these human figures are part and parcel of direct and immediate experience.

In contradistinction to this, we will find persons who go back very far in the scale of time or very far afield, geographically, or retreat into religion or mythology, peopling their created world with figures which cannot possibly be a part of their direct experience. For example, an "angel and a devil meeting outside Hell," is the response of a patient to this same blot. While such a response is not "bizarre" in the sense that it has no relation to reality (the inkblot is unquestionably more like an angel and a devil, since angels and devils are conceived of as having human forms, than it is like, say, the letter "M"), yet it will be seen that a different type of experience is drawn on when such an answer is given than, for example, your own of "two persons warming their hands over a brazier," which is something all of us have seen.

Physician: It is quite clear that "taking something" and "having something taken away" tells us about the roles played in life by those two particular boys, and it is safe to say that those particular actions were things that they had done, but I hate to tell you that I have never gone skiing, although I have always longed to be an expert athlete, and when my colleagues go, I feel out of it.

Psychologist: That is a very important distinction that you bring in. These "created puppets" in this miniature inkblot world are undoubtedly endowed *not only with the things which characterize our own actions*, but perhaps equally by our *fantasied actions*. Here you give a beautiful example of not having skied but often having wished that you had done so. Perhaps one should say that persons may sometimes not even be conscious of these fantasies until, through the medium of the inkblot, they are given their first tangible form. But, the point I wish to make is that the created actions are never the result of chance nor are they purely arbitrary. *At one level or another, either in fact or in fantasy, they tell us something about the individual's psychological actions.*

Human beings engaged in multifarious activities of almost infinite variety give us some of our most important insights in the inkblot tests. There is, for example, the "world" peopled almost exclusively with aggressive, overactive, pugnacious, fighting individuals. Sometimes these fantasied fighters reflect the individual's attitude toward others around him and sometimes they reflect inner conflict or fight within himself. Or, there may be a world peopled with figures who appear to menace the person who sees them. They have the expression of hostility or they are seen in threatening actions, they may be "about to kill." Conversely, there may be fantasied individuals who are happy, dancing, lovers about to embrace, friends shaking hands. Some persons create fantasied inkblot worlds where individuals may be found engaged in many different types of pursuits and in all walks of life, age, and sex. At the other extreme, there may be worlds created without the presence of a single human being. When this occurs, an important question arises as to why the patient chose to create a world neglecting one of the most obvious ingredients of the actual objective world in which he lives. For most of us it is difficult even to conceive of life without constant interaction with other people. When the fantasied world excludes others, when there is produced an environment from which people have been barred, we must ask why this particular creator is unwilling or unable to incorporate human beings.

In assessing how the world looks to any individual in terms of his own created inkblot human beings, it may be helpful to ask some questions like the following:

Does he create a world: Without others? Where others menace him? Where others are aggressive and belligerent? Where others are active but not aggressive? Where others are essentially passive? Where others are both active and passive? Of men only? Of women only? Of storybook or fantasied characters with which the individual cannot have had direct experience? Of a variety of characters with which the individual can have legitimately identified?

Physician: You sound like, or you remind me of, the old saying: "The world is so full of a number of things, I'm sure we should all be as happy as kings." I am wondering if this old saw is a sound one. Is the world of the happier, better adjusted individual characterized by a great number of different actions in which his imaginary population is engaged?

Psychologist: Very much so. Insofar as there are "normal" microscopic worlds, these worlds tend, as I shall show you later, to be variegated. This is understandable, since the objective world in which we live does not contain only one type of action which is irrevocably toward us nor are we realistically engaged in only one type of activity within this world. Thus when our microscopic worlds contain an excess of any one type of action either on the part of the individual or in terms of that which he conceives done to him, it is clear that he is overconcerned with some specific phase of adjustment or behavior. If, in the face of the variegated objective environment, his fantasied actions become too specialized, this indicates a curtailing of spontaneity and a restricting of the richness inherent in living.

When, in our discussion, we reach a point where I will show you how the responses in the Rorschach record are charted, summarized or assessed, you will find that the number of human beings who are seen and the type of actions in which they are engaged afford us important information when we try to reconstruct the experienced world of the perceiver. They represent the individual's capacity for fantasy and imagination.

At this point, because we have so much ground to cover, I am going to change your environment and subject you again to something new and meaningless. What do you see here, or what does this remind you of?

Physician: I am first struck by two animals, a sort of cross between a beaver and a sloth who are stepping out from a rock or the ground which is their natural habitat and are setting out on a voyage of exploration. One paw is already resting on higher ground and they are all set to climb up.

Psychologist: Let me stop you there so that you may contrast this answer of yours with one or two different mental constructs. Take, for example, "mutilated and horribly wounded animals plunging to their death." Or, take "timorous and hesitant sheep, cautiously approaching a hole in a fence through which they may venture." Would you like to make a comment about those three answers?

Physician: With your realization that I know nothing about the test, I would take a stab at it. Certainly, the individual who has made "mutilated animals" out of nothingness is more concerned with pain, shall I say, perhaps with death and destruction, than the man who makes his animals "cautiously approach a hole in a fence," or, for that matter, than I, myself, who sees them progressing on a voyage of discovery.

Psychologist: An excellent beginning and I might fill in the gaps for you. The man who saw hesitant sheep came for guidance prior to taking the step of getting married, something that he approached with great misgivings and insecurity. The response describing the mutilated animals plunging to their death was given by an extremely disturbed patient who had been sexually and emotionally traumatized to a very painful degree. Now, turning to your own answer, what do you think of in connection with a beaver?

Physician: "Busy as a beaver."

Psychologist: And, a sloth?

Physician: Why, slothfulness, ease, relaxation.

Psychologist: Isn't that a rather unusual combination, an extremely energetic and busy beaver and a lazy sloth? It might raise all sorts of questions in regard to your habits of work and play and your conflicts over relaxation and duty, or perhaps a solution to such a problem.

But, to continue, one of the most revealing facets of the individual comes from his handling of the animals which he creates in inkblots. Objectively, of course, the world is full of animals. Animals are slaughtered and eaten. Animals are kept as pets. Animals are beasts of burden. Animals are curiosities. Animals are completely controlled by human beings, or they may menace human beings. Animals are objects of highly technical research, and they are objects of art. A world, therefore, which is created "without animals" is a world with a gap in it. The individual who sees no animals has a blind spot to some of the aspects of the objective world. And thus we may ask, in the personal world of any given individual, what role is he going to make the animals play and which animals will he select to play these roles?

Physician: Would you say that my answer on this card and the other two answers which you have quoted were *similar* because we all saw some kind of animal, or essentially *different* because the animals were engaged in such very different activities?

Psychologist: There are both important similarities and important differences and this is where it may help you to see how such answers are recorded.

Here is a chart on which I have put down all the answers which had been mentioned in these few minutes. Usually such a chart is recorded, of course, for only one individual, but here we are interested in seeing where the different responses belong, given by you, the twin boys, and the patients I mentioned, in terms of some of the important perceptual categories. Look at Column One and you will find the Moving Human Beings recorded where *both* their similarity and their differences show up; the boy giving, the boy taking, and the men warming their hands.

Psychogram I
DEMONSTRATION OF SCORING

	M	FM	K	F	F—	Fc,c	C'	FC	CF	C+Csym.
14										
13										
12										
11										
10										
9										
8										
7										
6										
5										
4	Angel and Devil									
3	Boy giving up toy	Timorous sheep cautiously approaching fence	Submarine							
2	Boy taking toy	Horribly mutilated animals plunging to death	Piano							
1	Men warming their hands	Beaver-sloth stepping out			The Letter "M"		Snow on clothes	Brazier		
	Moving humans	Moving animals	Diffuse masses	Realistic objects	Unrealistic objects	Surfaces (hard - soft)	Blackness Whiteness	Objects Colored	Colored Masses	Color
	(M)	(FM)	(K)	(F)	(F—)	(Fc,c)	(C')	(FC)	(CF)	(C+Csym.)
	Inner life Fantasy	Drive "animal spirits"	Diffuse anxiety	Intellectual control Realistic	Distortions Unrealistic approach	Sensitivity Sensuality	Shyness Depression	Channelled relevant emotional experience	Strong emotions undirected	Diffuse emotionalism

In the next column, you will find the moving, timorous sheep, the moving mutilated animals, and the moving, exploring beaver-sloth. Disregarding the next two columns for the moment, we come to those epitomizing Unrealistic Objects, the letter "M," for example, the "piano," the "submarine," answers which bear no demonstrable resemblance to the shape of the inkblot that called them forth in the mind of the perceiver. Although we cannot trace their history in every case, these answers resulted from internal pressures, the *need* to see certain things, rather than from the utilization of the facts which were presented to the eye.

You will see that we have also entered here two other aspects of what you "created" on the first inkblot that you saw. The snow on the clothes of your skiers is listed over Blackness and Whiteness since the white aspect of the snow "determined," as we describe it, the reason for your seeing it. Your brazier, I have listed over Colored Objects since one of its outstanding characteristics is, of course, the glowing red coals which it contains.

Physician: From the fragment of this chart which exists at this moment, I can see that you will have a means of demonstrating graphically something you spoke about the other day, namely the *relative strength* of various pressures within the individual. For example, would I be right in assuming that if the column which you have called Unrealistic Objects became so high as to dominate all the others, that we would then be dealing with an individual out of contact with reality, someone who distorted meanings and was, therefore, psychotic?

Psychologist: That is precisely the reason why this particular chart was devised and why I am using it here. I want you to be able to distinguish the different types of responses, to see their similarities and their differences and subsequently to recognize the charts produced by recording the responses of patients with various types of psychological disturbances. As I have pointed out, a world which is dominated or overshadowed by any one of these particular columns will reflect certain outstanding characteristics of the individual's perception and thereby his behavior.

Physician: Now you have finally formulated something that has been bothering me. Why would you say "and thereby his behavior?" I can follow you when we are dealing with what a person sees and will agree that what a person sees in the inkblots must be related to what he sees in life. Or that which he constructs and makes out of nothingness will be found to be the same as what he sees or makes out of the world around him. But it seems to me a far cry from that to be able to make a psychiatric diagnosis or to claim that you can predict the type of behavior which will be found to characterize him.

Psychologist: May we shelve that very important question for one moment since I think it will involve us in quite a lengthy discussion? A satisfactory answer to this question is essential to a real understanding of the tests. Before we leave this fragmentary chart, I would like to say something about "worlds" which might be dominated by colored objects or color per se.

Looking at the meaning or significance of the "Colored Objects" and of "Color," you will see from the bottom line that in all instances these responses relate in some way or other to an individual's emotional makeup. It is important that this is not taken as an arbitrary statement but that the connection between color and emotional experience is formulated more clearly. Let me see if I can give you an example of what I mean. We are all likely to look out of the window as we wake up in the morning and make some comment on the kind of day. It may be "a lovely day" with brilliant sunshine, a fact which we will record with a lift of the spirits, or it may be dreary, even thunderously dark with an "ominous quality" to the clouds. Now its "loveliness" in terms of retinal stimulation is, of course, the brightness and the saturatedness of the colors which form a mosaic of separately excited rods and cones. Similarly, the "dreariness" of the horrible day is derived from less sharply differentiated and more monotone stimulation by the same objects on the same retinal areas. But from this pinpoint stimulation, we experience in the one case a feeling of exhilaration, and in the other, a feeling of depression or sadness. Thus, in a very primitive way, we react emotionally to the brightness and vividness of the coloring around us with a lifting of the spirits or, conversely, we register a mild depressive mood on the dark, dull days. Colors, differentiations, lights and shades, brightness and darkness and the contrasts between them impinge on us all the time. The brilliant and splendid world of the sunset becomes the somber world of twilight as the sun drops. All that has happened, however, in terms of the actual message that the eye receives, is that each pinpoint of stimulation on the retina receives a less intense ray of light.

The colored patches on the inkblot stimulate the retina in the same way as any brightly colored object. And one of the important things to know about an individual is to what extent he reacts to the situation which makes for basic gayness or somberness, to what extent he is receptive to color, or has, for some reason or other, interposed a shield between himself and its effect. Equally important is the extent to which he rushes at color, responding to it impulsively, letting it overpower him, letting it inundate and flood his world.

Physician: Would such an impulsive, emotional individual show answers in the columns you have called "Colored Masses and Color?"

Psychologist: Yes. And for such a person, these columns would be relatively weighted or stand relatively high in the pattern of the total graph. Merely to have answers in these columns does not mean that the personality is characterized by these particular emotional qualities. It becomes characteristic of an individual only insofar as too much of the total psychic energy that is available for expenditure gets charted into this type of perceptual activity.

Physician: What sort of responses qualify for tabulating here?

Psychologist: The general rule is that the less the *shape of the thing* is important for its selection, the more it will be evaluated in terms of color. For instance, you saw a brazier which is an *object of definite shape* in which burning coals (colored) are seen. If, however, you had just seen "fire," this would have lessened the element of form or shape. That is, you would have been much more impressed by the color so that the object in which the fire was burning became for you unimportant. But even fire has some shape. Hence we would have placed it in the column of Colored Masses — while just "redness" might have been placed in the column for Color alone.

There is really no hard and fast rule. We have to discover

in each instance more about the person's *experience* as he perceived and as he gave the answer.

Physician: But that, I suppose, would be one of those technical details that I don't have to concern myself with.

Psychologist: Right. These charts are intended to give you a general feel for the *kinds of things which we look for* in the responses. They are not meant to be instructive in the sense of teaching you how to administer the test or how to handle the findings. You will, however, have a much better chance of understanding the psychologist's reports if you can envisage the patient's productions, the "raw material," even in this rough way.

In our next session, I'll show you charts of various kinds. They will contrast the normal, neurotic, organic, and psychotic patient — not in order that you understand how or why each response was so charted, but to give you a visual impression of certain outstanding differences in the total patterns of performances.

Physician: There are a couple of columns here that you haven't mentioned. Realistic Objects, for example. Does that relate to those answers which you were previously describing as "good" or "justified"?

Psychologist: Yes. There is a large class of objects which are neither Moving Human Beings nor Moving Animals, which have no color and which are "determined" or prompted in the mind of the individual tested by certain areas of the blots simply because they have a similar outline or shape to some object that he knows. He is, in other ways, impressed by the form of the thing and justifiably so. These answers can be contrasted with those which are *not* justified by the form, the "crazy," unrealistic answers of the next column.

Physician: Looking at the first picture again — the thing that looked to me originally like a brazier for the burning coal now looks like the shape of a fox's head with the nose toward me.

Psychologist: Yes, and in seeing this, you completely disregard the color. Moreover, unlike your beaver-sloth animal that was actively engaged on a voyage of exploration, the fox's head is doing nothing. It is just the shape of his head. This is a good example of a realistic object, and in a chart, it would be so recorded.

Physician: That leaves us two columns still without comment. What are Diffuse Masses?

Psychologist: Supposing you saw, instead of your human beings, a shapeless cloud, or fog, mist, or smoke? That would be an answer with a quality of *diffuseness*, or formlessness, predominating.

Physician: And your Surfaces (Hard and Soft)?

Psychologist: Why did you speak of the men being in ski clothes?

Physician: It's almost as if I see the texture of their woolen suits.

Psychologist: And that is a "soft surface." Some aspects of perception might almost be likened to the eyes creeping into the ends of the fingertips and feeling or experiencing the surface of the blot. These fingertip-eyes react to smooth, polished surfaces or to very hairy, furry ones. Insofar as it seems to be this quality which determines why any particular likeness is selected, we record it here.

Physician: I see you equate this with both sensuality and sensibility. How come?

Psychologist: That's one of the inevitable shortcuts resulting from attempts to give bird's-eye-view explanations. A more detailed chart would have differentiated between them and, of course, they must be so differentiated for the psychologist. Actually, however, the discrepancy between sensuality and sensitivity is not as great as it may seem. They are found on a single continuum. The more the surface quality, regardless of form, swamps the eye of the beholder, the more he has become abandoned to the purely sensory-tactile quality of the thing he is looking at, the more his responses will tend to indicate sensuality. If, on the other hand, he endows a legitimate, realistic shape with surface qualities, he is allowing his fingertips to give him added information to his basic, intellectually determined facts. He is being sensitive to additional aspects of the gross shape which need not strike everybody. Your answer of the "woolen ski clothes" modifies or adds to the answer which is determined by the shape of the men and their characteristic pose of bending over the fire. If, however, you had seen nothing but "wool," your eyes would have been so much in your fingertips that they could not even see the other qualities which were equally, if not more, important.

Physican: Well, with the exception of these technicalities which, as you explain, cannot really be understood apart from a more careful study of how the patient was reacting, I think I understand something of these "perceptual ingredients" you originally spoke about. I get a feeling of the different ways in which these miniature psychological worlds can be constructed. But as always, I am full of more questions. For instance, would you have put a speed limit on my reactions had I been taking the tests in the usual manner, instead of as illustrative material?

Psychologist: Not a speed *limit*, but I would have to have taken note of your reaction times for, both absolutely and relatively, they would be of importance.

Physician: Meaning the time I took for the overall performance and the delays on certain answers?

Psychologist: Yes, some miniature psychological worlds are constructed extremely slowly and others very fast. For example, the organic patient seems to find the test a laborious and exhausting process. Each of the ten new environmental settings with which he is presented is equally difficult for him. He tries every time to get his bearings, to discover something to be able to tell the examiner and fulfill the test instructions. He is painfully aware of his own slowness, aware of his own difficulties, and this awareness is part of his world. Hence the task for him is an unpleasant one and his distress is evidenced clearly.

Sometimes, if this distress becomes too acute, we will find him so eager to terminate the experience that he will substitute a false answer for a real one. That is, although he really sees nothing, let us say, in Blot #2, he will repeat an answer that he has given on Blot #1, repeat a description of a previous environment, not because he considers it relevant, but in order to get out of a tension-producing situation.

At the opposite pole from these slowly and painfully constructed psychological worlds, we find the torrent of images which flow in an undifferentiated stream. In some patients the scene is shifted again and again and in the space of sixty seconds, perhaps some twenty different entities have been built up, and as quickly lost.

Physician: Lost?

Psychologist: Yes. When the patient is asked to point out any of his answers, it will have already disappeared before he can put a finger on it or outline it for the examiner to see.

In general, we may say that when a world is constructed extremely slowly, it will have another characteristic, namely that of *irreversibility* or *lack of flexibility*. One image constructed, one object seen, and there is little chance of the blot undergoing a new organization or having a new focal point, so that it can then possess other characteristics and appear as other objects. On the other hand, in the worlds which are constructed with lightning speed, there is too great flexibility, and we find this *fluctuating* quality. It becomes hard for this builder to keep any one object, unit, or area stable. Things, as it were, melt into each other and grow out of each other.

Extreme slowness and extreme speed, complete lack of flexibility and a too plastic fluctuation — these can be considered as end points in two closely related, but nonetheless distinct scales. For it is possible to be slow in construction, but also to be able to be somewhat flexible. And it is possible to be flooded with ever changing impressions, but nonetheless to maintain a relative stability in regard to each construct. It has seemed to me that this quality of *stability-despite-speed* is one of the differentiating features between the borderline psychotic and the individual we call "gifted."

Physician: You've obviously been talking up till now

about absolute speed. What is the significance in timing each response?

Psychologist: Had you been taking the test systematically instead of just for illustrative material, I would have been interested in seeing in what areas you are thrown off balance or thrown out of your usual and, let us say, natural rate of production. Where do you block? Where do ideas and responses fail you? You may, for example, be doing very well until part of one of the blots is colored. This color, this introduction of emotional stimulation, may momentarily set you back on your heels either because "your mind goes blank" or because you consciously repress certain associations which you do not wish to reveal. One of the most common areas of blocking comes when the card which has obvious sexual connotations is presented. Sometimes the combination of delay and an unusually poor or unjustified answer following "blocking" gives us an interesting clue to some of the more specific features of a patient's difficulty.

Physician: So much for the time element. There was something else I thought of asking you as I was looking at one of those inkblots. Oh, yes — does it make any difference if I give my answer in terms of the whole inkblot picture as I did when I saw the skiers warming their hands over the brazier with the colored lights behind, or when I was interested in only part of the picture, as, for instance, my animals out on a voyage of discovery? I noticed that when I saw them, I was uninterested in or really disregarded other parts of the blot.

Psychologist: The extent to which you utilize, in your responses, the whole blot, large parts of the blot, or very small parts of the blot, is a very important factor in assessing the record technically and in understanding individual mental organization. For example, let us consider how the world looks to a patient who saw nothing in Figure I except "an icicle" in the small protuberance on the "foot," and continued, throughout the ten inkblots, to pay attention only to such minute areas. What would you say about how the world looked to such an individual?

Physician: Well, offhand I am reminded of the statement that some people don't see the woods for the trees, only in this instance, this fellow probably wouldn't even see the tree. He'd be more apt to be staring at the moss on the stem.

Psychologist: That will do well for a start. Here is a hypothetical person who is going to have difficulties because the meanings he finds in life are going to be so different from those of others around him. He will not see the interconnectedness of things. He will be so glued to the small tasks that larger issues will completely escape him and this, in turn, is bound to bring about a certain psychological isolation, for there will not be many people with whom he can communicate in terms of these interests based on minutiae.

Physician: But isn't the individual who never saw any of the small areas at all and who dealt only in terms of the total pictures, likely to be too much of a theorist who never got down to brass tacks or to handling the specific situations?

Psychologist: Undoubtedly. The individual who is psychologically incapable of breaking up the total experience, who is unable to pay attention to any details, either in real life or in the blots, is just as likely to have psychological difficulties. For the most part, however, we are dealing in terms of *proportions* rather than all or none values. There are clearly people whose forte lies, intellectually, in being able to plan, theorize, generalize. Such basic perceptual equipment, reflected in the test, can be utilized constructively, provided it is alleviated, shall we say, by the capacity to handle the more concrete and specific details of life. Conversely, the individual who spontaneously puts great emphasis on the scrutiny of tiny areas can turn this basic mode of operation into extremely constructive channels. Many types of research, for example, medical and otherwise, require an extraordinary capacity for relentless and detailed observations.

Physician: That I can well understand, and I imagine since balanced proportions are so important in this kind of testing, there must be some optimum distribution whereby people are neither obsessively interested in small details nor lost in vague generalizations.

Before you stop this discussion, I do want one of my earlier questions answered. You see, you no longer have to convince me that individuals create out of nothingness perceptual worlds which reflect their own meanings, and I can see by your graphs that you have a way of charting which properties of perception are dominant in an individual's make-up. But now comes a gap in my mind. How can you tell how people act? What's the relation of seeing to doing?

Psychologist: I don't believe you are as far from understanding this as you think, but it is a difficulty which bothers many people and, in teaching, I recently hit on a device which I think may help you bridge the gap for yourself as it did with my students.

Let us take again the animals which you saw in Figure II
— the animals which were a combination of a beaver and
a sloth. Now all I have to ask you to do is to take them (in
imagination) off the small-sized inkblot picture, blow them
up to life-size and put them in a room. You would then
act toward these life-size animals in a way that made sense
in terms of what they were. For instance, you would not
be terrified of them or run out of the room. But a patient
who had seen in that same area "a frightening and menacing monster" would, if confronted with a life-size model,
behave in a different way. He *would* run away from it *and
it would make sense for him to run away from something
that he perceived as frightening and menacing.* In other
words, behavior is directly adapted to and intimately connected with that which is perceived. "Nothingness" for this
individual was organized into something frightening, *and it
is perfectly sensible to be frightened of the frightening!
Thus, I can predict that his actions will be relevant to the
world he constructs.*

Physician: What you are really saying is that if all action
is so intimately bound up with and can only arise from the
situation as it is perceived, then all behavior even if "maladjusted" from the standpoint of the majority, is nonetheless
adjusted to the situation *as perceived by the individual.*

Psychologist: Exactly, and so in studying "maladjusted"
behavior, it is important to get back behind the actions and
see what sort of private psychological world made the individual respond as he did. *Perception and action are intimately connected and action cannot be ill-adapted to that
which is perceived.*

And now let me pull together some of these findings. For

an understanding of the Rorschach Test, one must always be aware that the individual is a whole person, such that his activities on the perceptual level give information about his behavior. Or put it this way, the pattern of how he proceeds visually mirrors the patterning of other types of psychological experiences and actions. Thus, it is not purely accidental that the individual who visually breaks down the inkblot pictures into innumerable small fragments is someone for whom in life the broad, underlying, interconnected meanings are lacking, so that his experience becomes a mosaic, piecemeal, a disjointed train of events. The different worlds as experienced by different individuals lead to behavior which is appropriate for the world as they experience it. Thus we are justified in making some predictions about behavior from what the patient sees. Conversely, where the behavioral pattern is well known we may catch a glimpse through the inkblot worlds of the *types of distorted experiences* which are giving rise to the disturbed behavior.*

---

* The two illustrations of inkblots used in this chapter are Cards #3 and #8, taken from the Harrower Inkblot Series, published by Grune and Stratton Co., New York City. Use of the Rorschach Inkblots themselves would violate the copyright. This series of inkblots, however, has been equated with the Rorschach and is used frequently as an alternative set.

Contrasting Psychological Worlds

Psychologist: In summarizing some of our discussion to date, I think it would be fair to state that you now see that the meaningless inkblots provide a kind of plastic material whereby the mind can create a miniature world in conformity with its own needs. From these ten meaningless inkblot pictures, different individual worlds are fashioned which appear as strikingly distinct and as unique as each of the individuals who fashion them. In getting information about a patient through the scrutiny of how the world looks to him, it became clear that we need a method whereby the characteristics of the person as a particular type can be distinguished from those aspects which were essentially personal or unique. We need a way in which we can group and order an individual's psychic productions. The chart you and I constructed together showed one way in which this could be done.

I have here eight charts, eight "patterned psychological worlds," which I will show you in contrasting pairs. As you look at them, you might keep in mind questions such as these: Is this a rich world filled with many psychic items, or is it an impoverished one? How realistic is this individual? To what extent do his productions fly in the face of reality, being molded by his own internal needs? To what extent does color overrun this world indicating undue emotionality or preoccupation with moods and effects?

For our first contrasting pair, I should like you to look at what I have called *The Moderate and Variegated World of the Undisturbed Person* and compare it with *The Empty and Stereotyped World of the Organic Patient.*

What would be your first reaction as to the obvious differences between these two productions?

Physician: It's clear that your so-called "normal" is a much more productive person than the organic patient. As a matter of fact, if I understand your diagram correctly, you have put three organic patients on the same page, so it takes three of them to equal the normal's productions.

Psychologist: Correct.

Physician: Then, I would like to use your words "variegated" as opposed to "stereotyped." As I read over the things which constitute the world of the "normal," it is quite clear that he is reflecting experiences drawn from a much wider range of living. Putting it the other way, your organic patients seem to get an idea and harp on it endlessly. One is completely preoccupied with bats, another with birds and butterflies, and the third with ink!

Psychologist: This characteristic, which I spoke of briefly yesterday, is known as perseveration. It is one of the most important features of the empty and stereotyped world produced by the organic patient. It would seem that persons handicapped in this way, psychologically, keep on

Psychogram II

THE MODERATE AND VARIEGATED WORLD OF THE UNDISTURBED PERSON

#	M	FM	K	F	F–	Fc,c	C'	FC	CF	C+Csym.
14										
13										
12	2 priests standing, hands upraised									
11	Man receiving a blessing									
10	2 clowns clapping hands									
9	2 people dancing together									
8	Guards, back to back									
7	2 waiters dancing together			Face of a cat				Red stocking caps		
6	2 warlocks dancing around	2 bears dancing noses touching		Head of an ox				Red bow		
5	Ballet dancers in flowing costumes	Bears		Head of a moose without horns				A red moth		
4	2 old ladies gossiping	Agile creatures climbing		View of female parts				Red butterfly		
3	Dancers	Little bugs quarreling		Insect		Feathers		Scene in nature		
2	2 imps exploding out of container	Poodles posing	Greenish smoke	Phallic symbol		Indian headwear		Sea creatures		
1	Sorcerers' tall caps	Unicorns leaping towards each other	Smoke rising	Heads of beetles		Shaggy fur		Green caterpillars	Ice cream	Flash of fire
	Moving humans	Moving animals	Diffuse masses	Realistic objects	Unrealistic objects	Surfaces (hard – soft)	Blackness Whiteness	Objects Colored	Colored Masses	Color
	(M)	(FM)	(K)	(F)	(F–)	(Fc,c)	(C')	(FC)	(CF)	(C+Csym.)
	Inner life Fantasy Drive "animal spirits"		Diffuse anxiety	Intellectual control Realistic	Distortions Unrealistic approach	Sensitivity Sensuality	Shyness Depression	Channeled relevant emotional experience	Strong emotions undirected	Diffuse emotionalism

Psychogram III

THE EMPTY AND STEREOTYPED WORLD OF THE ORGANIC PATIENT

CASE III

	Moving humans	Moving animals	Diffuse masses	Realistic objects	Unrealistic objects	Surfaces (hard-soft)	Blackness Whiteness	Objects Colored	Colored Masses	Color
2										
1										

CASE II

	Moving humans	Moving animals	Diffuse masses	Realistic objects	Unrealistic objects	Surfaces (hard-soft)	Blackness Whiteness	Objects Colored — Bow	Colored Masses	Color
				Bat	Bat					
8					Another butterfly					
7					Butterfly					
6				Another bird outspread wings and paw	Open bird, outspread wings					
5				Open wings	Birds spreading out wings					
4				Paws	Another bird					
3				Body, wings of a bird	Another bird					
2				2 heads of 2 animals	Part of ostrich head					
1				A bat	Indicative of airplane					

CASE I

	Moving humans	Moving animals	Diffuse masses	Realistic objects	Unrealistic objects	Surfaces (hard-soft)	Blackness Whiteness	Objects Colored	Colored Masses	Color
3		Couple of dogs					Using up some ink			Bunch of blue spots
2		Couple of dogs					Black ink			Bunch of red spots
1							Spit ink			Red ink

	Moving humans	Moving animals	Diffuse masses	Realistic objects	Unrealistic objects	Surfaces (hard-soft)	Blackness Whiteness	Objects Colored	Colored Masses	Color
Symbol	(M)	(FM)	(K)	(F)	(F−)	(Fc,c)	(C')	(FC)	(CF)	(C+Csym.)
Meaning	Inner life Fantasy	Drive "animal spirits"	Diffuse anxiety	Intellectual control Realistic	Distortions Unrealistic approach	Sensitivity Sensuality	Shyness Depression	Channeled relevant emotional experience	Strong emotions undirected	Diffuse emotionalism

with one response regardless of its adequacy in subsequent situations. It becomes, one might say, the lesser of two evils; to repeat an answer is better than to fail and to produce nothing at all.

Physician: I am struck by a few other things. Your "normal" individual seems to have as his strongest suits those answers which relate to "channeled and relevant emotional experiences" and "inner fantasy life." This normal fellow must be both imaginative and warm if I may take these findings at face value. But the organic patients, Cases I, II, and III, have no inner fantasy life recorded at all and their emotional responsiveness seems to be either diffuse or lacking.

Psychologist: This is a perfectly valid deduction. Perhaps I might amplify it somewhat in this way. Since we consider constructive imagination and fantasy, on the one hand, and a well developed emotional life, on the other, as two indications of psychological maturity, one way of describing the three records epitomizing the world of the organic would be to say that he is living in, or constructing, a much more primitive undifferentiated world, in addition to its being both impoverished and stereotyped.

Physician: As I look more closely at the three examples of the organic patient, I am struck now by a dissimilarity between the three records, despite the class or group characteristics which were easily contrasted with the normal fellow.

Psychologist: I may be able to throw some light on that. The first case is perhaps the "purest" example one could find. This sixteen-year-old girl suffered a birth injury and encephalograms reveal large areas of diffuse damage and atrophy. Case II, on the other hand, is more complex, this being recorded clinically as the "possibility of a paranoid schizophrenic illness superimposed on a deteriorating organic process." You will note that in this instance, there is a very high proportion of unrealistic objects seen, which, while they are not bizarre in themselves, bear no legitimate relationship to the blot or parts of the blot that elicited them as responses.* Case III, also with a large area of demonstrable cerebral damage, is described as a behavior problem and this, I think, you could deduce from the ingredients which make up his psychologically constructed world. The extent to which diffuse emotional reactions must permeate it and the lack of intellectual control, together with his depression and moodiness, make very unsatisfactory psychological ingredients for living.

Keeping these contrasting cases in mind — the "normal" and the organic — let us move on to consider two other types of psychological worlds. The first I have called *The World of Too-Compelling Fantasy of the Withdrawn Individual*; the second, *The Emotionally Invaded World of the Hysterical Individual*.

---

* The arrangement of the answers in these charts may not always be clear to the reader since the reason for a response appearing under a given heading rests on technical details which, in this type of presentation, we have sought to avoid. It is impossible, for example, to demonstrate *why* any particular answer has been considered as one with an "unjustified form." This must rest on the examiner's appraisal of the response *with reference to that part of the inkblot which elicits it*. In the previous chapter, we give examples of such unrealistic ways of reacting to the meaningless material (responses "M," "Piano," "Submarine") and such examples must serve for subsequent cases.

The inclusion of some animals in the column pertaining to the *shape* of the object rather than in that which epitomizes the animal in action is due to the fact that in these instances the response denied life to the animal and was a representation of the outline of an animal, rather than the animal as a living entity.

Psychogram IV
THE WORLD OF TOO-COMPELLING FANTASY OF THE WITHDRAWN INDIVIDUAL

	M	FM	K	F	F-	Fc,c	C'	FC	CF	C+Csym.
20										
19	2 children feeding									
18	Man chucking under chin									
17	Woman with painted fingernails									
16	Children making faces			The skeleton						
15	People back to back			Pectoral girdle						
14	Fat people dancing			Head of a deer						
13	Knock-kneed bat man			Horse heads						
12	People hiding behind cloak			Butterfly						
11	Dancing girls			Another bat						
10	People asking for alms			Head of a lizard						
9	Queen in Alice in Wonderland	Toads running		Bat						
8	A clown	Spiders running		Tremendous feet						
7	Waiters pulling something apart	Monkey holding out hand		Sting ray						
6	Girl putting foot in water	Lizards climbing		2 little heads						
5	Negroes, arms pointing	2 scotties		Head of a camel						
4	People trying to outdo each other	2 little dogs		Toe nails						
3	2 humorous characters	2 poodles		Pelvic girdle						
2	Dancers without heads	Birds playing pat-a-cake		More faces		Totem pole				
1	A sitting Buddha	2 bears dancing		2 gargoyle faces		Bear rug				
	Moving humans	Moving animals	Diffuse masses	Realistic objects	Unrealistic objects	Surfaces (hard – soft)	Blackness Whiteness	Objects Colored	Colored Masses	Color
	(M)	(FM)	(K)	(F)	(F—)	(Fc,c)	(C')	(FC)	(CF)	(C+Csym.)
	Inner life Fantasy	Drive "animal spirits"	Diffuse anxiety	Intellectual control Realistic	Distortions Unrealistic approach	Sensitivity Sensuality	Shyness Depression	Channeled relevant emotional experience	Strong emotions undirected	Diffuse emotionalism

Psychogram V
THE EMOTIONALLY INVADED WORLD OF THE HYSTERICAL INDIVIDUAL

(Tally columns numbered 14, 13, 12, 11, 10, 9, 8, 7, 6, 5, 4, 3, 2, 1 — all blank.)

Level	M	FM	K	F	F−	Fc,c	C′	FC	CF	C+Csym.
8								Someone's insides	Someone's insides	
7				Cat's whiskers					Colored fountain	
6				Bat					Something dyed	
5				Animal's head					Leaf, changing color	
4				Skeleton		Costume jewelry			Colored litmus paper	
3				Insect		Leaf from tree			Vagina	Colored lights
2				Butterfly		Leopard skin			Batik design	Colors in puddle
1	Fire dancers	Animals		Bat	Map	Pelt of animal		Caterpillar		Splotches of ink
	Moving humans	Moving animals	Diffuse masses	Realistic objects	Unrealistic objects	Surfaces (hard-soft)	Blackness Whiteness	Objects Colored	Colored Masses	Color
	(M)	(FM)	(K)	(F)	(F−)	(Fc,c)	(C′)	(FC)	(CF)	(C+Csym.)
	Inner life Fantasy	Drive "animal spirits"	Diffuse anxiety	Intellectual control Realistic	Distortions Unrealistic approach	Sensitivity Sensuality	Shyness Depression	Channeled relevant emotional experience	Strong emotions undirected	Diffuse emotionalism

The miniature world of the withdrawn individual, a young man in his early twenties, as can be seen instantly, is overloaded with the type of response that reflects preoccupation with an active life of fantasy. What else would you say characterizes this particular psychic construction?

Physician: There just aren't many responses at all which reflect an awareness of or responsiveness to those emotional effects of color.

Psychologist: That is extremely important and it stands to reason that someone who is so wrapped up in himself and so unaware of emotions or unable to respond emotionally is in danger of failing to come to grips with the real world and of slipping out of contact. While this admittedly is a grave danger, it must be noted, on the other hand, that there is a complete absence of all those responses which indicate any kind of "distortion of reality," an absence, that is, of unrealistic forms and shapes. So, we could say that the pressures of this boy's internal needs, and they are very great, are not of a kind as to force him to *misrepresent* the qualities of objective reality.

Physician: Perhaps it's the counterpart of what you have been saying, but I would say that he has better than average realistic approach. The column representing realistic objects is quite high. He also seems to have a lively animal world, but I wouldn't know what that means in this case.

Psychologist: It's unquestionably an asset. The fact that for him the animal kingdom (with its symbolic portrayal of instinctive life) is alive and active is a healthy sign, and one of the assets which may be used to break up the extraordinary hold that fantasy has on this individual.

Physician: In looking at the imaginary people of this boy's universe, I am struck by the almost indefinite number of roles, both male and female, active and passive, with which they are endowed.

Psychologist: True. It is as if he can play, mentally, a great variety of roles, but such variety may become dangerous when there are no emotional outlets. This young man does not live out consistently any one type of action, but, in the role of fantasy, sees himself in many different roles.

Physician: How does this patient feel? What's wrong with him as far as he is concerned?

Psychologist: In his own words, he describes his complaints as "feeling as if he would explode unless he goes off by himself." This is understandable from the type of world he produces, for his fantasy cannot be subdued, nor can it be channeled outward. Hence it *competes* with the tasks of reality, necessitating a withdrawal into solitude to prevent the explosion. This gives us an interesting insight into the relation of fantasy and withdrawal. It is not so much that the isolated and withdrawn individual *fills his solitude with fantasy life*, but rather that the fantasy life in and of itself is an active and compelling ingredient demanding attention so that literally, in order to cope with it, the individual is forced into seeking solitude.

Physician: And how is he pigeonholed psychiatrically?

Psychologist: He is not considered psychotic. I think "a markedly schizoid individual" was the diagnostic label.

In striking contrast to this, almost the mirror-image, is *The Emotionally Invaded World of the Hysterical Indi-*

vidual. Here it will be seen that the distribution of psychic energy is weighted almost entirely in terms of those responses motivated or influenced by color. There is an absence of, or more likely repression of, both active fantasy and the biological animal drive. This patient is also in good contact with reality (the realistic approach far outweighs the unrealistic distortions) but there is too much emotion to be handled successfully. Clinically, she was diagnosed as "conversion hysteria." She responded well to therapy, and when retested two years later showed quite a remarkable redistribution of psychic energies. Her world was no longer overrun with emotions; men and women engaged in various types of activities had been allowed admittance in the world of fantasy.

In describing the inkblot productions of psychotic patients, I have chosen two different types of records. The one might be called *The Bizarre and Frightening World*, the other, *The Unrealistic World*. If you turn back for a moment and read again the responses of the *Withdrawn Individual*, you notice there is nothing of an essentially bizarre or fantastic nature in his productions; the world in which he lives is still the recognizable one. In contrast to this, the charted record of this particular psychotic patient affords illustration of a distorted and chaotic miniature world where weird and, in fact, "crazy" ideas are expressed. Human beings have strange characteristics which never actually occur. For example, "breasts coming out of their shoulders." Animals are engaged in sadistic mutilating activities, "animals biting on a penis." Parts of the body assume bizarre functions, "penises eating the eyes out of a rabbit." Overall, there is a frightening and horrendous attitude, "awful things coming up out of the ocean." Again, in contrast to the *Withdrawn Individual's* lack of response to color, this patient reacts to color in a manner that is unrestrained and inarticulated. He is unable to channel his emotions successfully. He lives in a miniature universe where things have lost their proper place and function. That he is diagnosed clinically as "frankly paranoid and psychotic" is not surprising. (Psychogram VI)

Although the second psychotic patient has a few strange concepts such as "colored psycho traits" and "dilations," his world is less bizarre than it is unrealistic. The abnormality of the record in this instance is carried structurally, rather than in the flavor of its content. Note the extent to which unrealistic thinking predominates. Look at the amount of strong undirected emotions, the lack of rational perspective and control. These together with the absence of all capacity for inner life and the diffuse anxiety makes this patient a tragically vulnerable individual. (Psychogram VII)

Physician: Should I expect then that all psychotic individuals would construct a miniature world like one or the other of these two samples?

Psychologist: That, unfortunately, would be a gross oversimplification. In all attempts to teach, one must take clear-cut and unmistakable specimens as a starting point. The charts I have shown you serve as illustrations of how the psychological worlds constructed out of the inkblot material vary both in respect to the strength of the various psychological components and in the flavor, content, or quality of the actual responses themselves. There are few hard and fast lines and very few occasions where snap judgments can be made. Just to begin to show you some of the difficulties, let me introduce in conclusion, two more cases. These, I have

Psychogram VI

THE BIZARRE AND FRIGHTENING WORLD OF THE PSYCHOTIC

#	(M)	(FM)	(m)	(K)	(F)	(F—)	(Fc,c)	(C')	(FC)	(CF)	(C+Csym.)
14											
13		Penises eating the eyes out of a rabbit									
12		A vagina reaching up									
11		Animals biting on a penis									
10		2 proud yellow lions									
9		The dove of peace sitting on a penis									
8		Bloody animals prowling				Awful looking claws					
7		Animals dancing				Vagina and anus					
6		2 butterflies trying to keep them from hurting				Vagina					
5		Elephants dancing on a butterfly				Clippers goes back to woman					
4	2 woman looking at each other	Awful thing coming out of ocean			2 penises					Animals drowned in blood	An explosion
3	Woman with legs spread	Horrible sea animal			2 legs					Bloody skinned animals	The height of intercourse
2	2 men foppishly dressed	Horrible sea animal			Clippers where sex organs should be	A penis with bat's wings growing out of it				Bloody male sex organs, also menstrual	Blood dropping on the floor
	Woman with breasts coming out of shoulders		Bats that will envelop you	Clouds	Ugly bat	Sex organs with eyes and feelers	Bearskin rug	Maps, ice-bound		Female sex organs	Blood again
	Moving humans	Moving animals			Realistic objects	Unrealistic objects	Surfaces (hard - soft)	Blackness Whitness	Objects Colored	Colored Masses	Color
	(M)	(FM)		(K)	(F)	(F—)	(Fc,c)	(C')	(FC)	(CF)	(C+Csym.)
	Inner life Fantasy	Drive "animal spirits"	Diffuse anxiety	Diffuse masses	Intellectual control Realistic	Distortions Unrealistic approach	Sensitivity Sensuality	Shyness Depression	Channeled relevant emotional experience	Strong emotions undirected	Diffuse emotionalism

Psychogram VII
THE UNREALISTIC WORLD OF THE PSYCHOTIC

#	Moving humans (M) Inner life Fantasy	Moving animals (FM) Drive "animal spirits"	Diffuse masses (K) Diffuse anxiety	Realistic objects (F) Intellectual control Realistic	Unrealistic objects (F—) Distortions Unrealistic approach	Surfaces (hard-soft) (Fc,c) Sensitivity Sensuality	Objects Colored (FC) Channeled relevant emotional experience	Blackness Whiteness (C') Shyness Depression	Colored Masses (CF) Strong emotions undirected	Color (C+Csym.) Diffuse emotionalism
14										
13					Bones lying around	Blue Ice				
12					Iliac	Egg with blood clots				
11					Heart	Maps				
10					Female organ and kidney	Sherberts				
9					Map	Quartz				
8					Brains	Sherberts				
7					Backbone	Ice Cream				
6					Rivers	Kidney				
5					Backbone	Part of Heart				
4		Rodents climbing			"Dilations"	Woman's organs				Colored glass
3		Monkeys looking	Clouds		Dead cow	Kidney				A "psychotrait"
2		Apes holding	Clouds		Scorpion					Blood
1		Monster horrible	Clouds		Spider	Woman's organs	Horrible green snakes	Mountains	Colored Masses	A conflict

described as *The Impoverished World of the Deeply Neu-rotic Personality*. (Psychogram VIII)

Physician: At first glance, I would have thought that they were organic patients.

Psychologist: You would be right in the sense that the lack of productivity or impoverishment comes very close to what we have described as *The Empty and Stereotyped World of the Organic Patient*. However, investigation of these records will show some important differences. The chief difference will lie in the lack of the perseverative quality, and in each case a slightly larger number of varied types of responses are given. Concerning the first of these cases, the psychiatric summary, which reached me from the referring physician, is as follows: "This is an extraordinary development failure in an individual with multiple concealed phobias who has, throughout his life, been so protected he cannot face up to any of them and, therefore, has not been forced to develop any obsessional compulsive patterns beyond the empty inertia of his entire life. There is a lack of investment in any emotional relationship in the outside world rather than a distortion of objective relations. The entire world is a vague and unformulated threat to him. The result is a deeply neurotic personality, result of a total failure of emotional maturation for which we have no specific name." A somewhat similar description clinically, was given for the other case.

Physician: And what did *you* say about this man? How would you point up these findings which show in the chart?

Psychologist: These cases were done "blind" and my summary turned out to be very similar to that derived from the psychiatric interview. In one case, the report read:

Psychogram VIII
THE IMPOVERISHED WORLD OF THE DEEPLY NEUROTIC PERSONALITY

	(M)	(FM)	(K)	(F)	(F-)	(Fc,c)	(C')	(FC)	(CF)	(C+Csym.)
CASE II 4										
3				Another insect						
2				Some specimen of insect						
1	Moving humans	2 rats trying to climb a tree		Insect	Butterfly			Flower		
				Bat	2 birds					
(category)	Moving humans	Moving animals	Diffuse masses	Realistic objects	Unrealistic objects	Surfaces (hard‑soft)	Blackness Whiteness	Objects Colored	Colored Masses	Color
CASE I 4				2 heads						
3		Various fanciful forms of animals		2 headless characters						
2		2 animals		Bat						
1		Some horrible serpent		2 sorts of caricatures	Some sort of starfish	Skin of animal				Bad dream
(category)	Moving humans	Moving animals	Diffuse masses	Realistic objects	Unrealistic objects	Surfaces (hard‑soft)	Blackness Whiteness	Objects Colored	Colored Masses	Color
	(M)	(FM)	(K)	(F)	(F-)	(Fc,c)	(C')	(FC)	(CF)	(C+Csym.)
	Inner life Fantasy	Drive "animal spirits"	Diffuse anxiety	Intellectual control Realistic	Distortions Unrealistic approach	Sensitivity Sensuality	Shyness Depression	Channeled relevant emotional experience	Strong emotions undirected	Diffuse emotionalism

"The total picture here is a very discouraging one in the sense that all tests show regression to a very primitive and undifferentiated level of performance. His disturbances have invaded all areas, leaving him with a minimum of human qualities, either intellectual or emotional, with which to function. He is perilously isolated with nothing to hold on to. While he clearly needs to be supported, it is questionable whether he can establish the type of emotional relationship that he so badly needs."

Physician: To go back for a moment to the first cases you showed me, what was the reason for the referral of your "normal" individual, and why do the organic patients need to be tested?

Psychologist: The "normal" individual was a candidate for a rather important position requiring both imagination and the capacity to get along well with other people. It has become a practice in some business firms to refer candidates for this type of psychological appraisal when an important position has to be filled. In the case of this man, since all the other tests were as impressively "normal" as this one, we strongly recommended that he be accepted for the position.

In regard to the organic patients, in Cases II and III, a question had come up as to the advisability of their remaining hospitalized rather than returning to the family setting. At the time of the examination, it appeared from the tests that over and above the deficiency resulting from the organic condition, the possibility of an underlying psychosis in the one case, and the clearly delineated behavior problem in the other, resulted in the suggestion that they remain hospitalized at least for the time being.

Physician: Would you expect me to utilize these charts myself?

Psychologist: No. I devised them so that they might constitute a transitional stage for you between the psychologist's specialized notations, on the one hand, and his "writing about the patient," on the other. You may remember that we discussed the physician's lack of exposure to the "actual raw material" when it came to psychological findings;* whereas in contrast, in your hospital conferences, you and the radiologist, or you and your electroencephalographer, looked at the raw material together in these respective fields. It has been my aim to produce something comparable in psychology to X-ray films or electroencephalographic tracings in order that a more meaningful type of discussion of the patient's psychological problems could take place.

Physician: Can you tell me how the shorthand notations would appear in these cases?

Psychologist: Surely. Take *The Empty and Stereotyped World of the Organic Patient* and select Case I. This would read R5 W4 D1 F2 F-2 FC1 P2 A4 Ad0 M:C=0:.5. Interpreting again, we would have five total responses (R5) of which four employed the whole blot in the constructing of the response (W4) and one response related to a large detail (D1). Two of the responses had legitimate realistic form (F2) and two were constructed and unrealistically (F-2). One response involved use of both form and color (FC1). Two responses would be "popular"; that is, given frequently by a cross section of the total population (P2).

---

* See page 40.

There were four animal responses (A4), but no animal details (Ad0). The ratio of the human movement responses reflecting the inner fantasy life to those responses that reflect susceptibility to color is 0:.5.

Physician: Well, I'm glad it's not my responsibility to assess these records, but I would be able now, I think, if my psychological colleague were to give me a patient's responses displayed in this way, to be somewhat more aware of his perceptual and conceptual patterns of experience. I do get the "feel" of the psychotic patient's bizarre type of answers and could distinguish it from the monosyllabic record of the organic case and the more variegated performance of your "normal" candidate for the position. I would also obviously be struck by that excessive dwelling in the world of fantasy of the schizoid boy. Let me see if I can say it correctly. He would have a ratio of inner life to emotional responsiveness of 19:0, if I am not mistaken!

Psychologist: We will have you taking and scoring Rorschach records before long! Seriously, however, it may be of interest to you sometime to give the test yourself to a willing victim. Not with the idea of coming up with the answers or making diagnostic decisions, but to see — even at a superficial level — how very differently people respond. There is no substitute for experiencing first hand the enormous variety that can occur in the worlds that we constructed from these ten meaningless blots.

▄▄▟▟▟▟▟▟▟▟▟▟▟▟▟▟▟▟▟▟▟▟▟▟▟▟▟▟▟▟▟▟▟▟▟▟▟▄▄

There's More to it Than the I.Q.

Psychologist: I think you told me that you had taken an intelligence test. You have had the experience, then, of being asked a direct question and having to supply the correct answer, sometimes within a time limit, so I won't have to put you through your paces again.

Physician: As I remember it, I was asked some very simple questions, like what was a thermometer and what does the heart do. I had to do some mental arithmetic, among other things, and make little designs out of colored blocks.

Psychologist: That sounds like the Wechsler-Bellevue and what you remember of it will do excellently as a frame of reference for our discussion. To my mind such an intelligence test is an essential part of every clinical examination, regardless of how expert the psychologist is in the use of the projective techniques or how firm his belief in their efficacy, for it provides several different kinds of information.

Physician: Well, I think I know Number 1. It gives you

the "I.Q.," something your projective techniques don't go in for. But, to tell you the truth, I don't know what a good I.Q. is, nor do I know what I'd do with the information if you told me one of my patients was a potential genius.

Psychologist: The I.Q. locates the individual at some point on a quantitative scale. This is easily communicated and it is a good starting point for a psychological evaluation. Sometimes this objective information conflicts with the impression the individual has given clinically, a fact which in itself may alter the physician's approach to him. This quantitative base line varies from mentally defective scores, I.Q.'s of below 67, though borderline defective scores, I.Q.'s of 68 to 79, through low-average scores, 79 to 90, average, 91 to 110, high-average, 111 to 119, superior, from 120 to 127, and very superior, 128 and over. For adults, this "over" brings them up to a maximum of approximately 150.

Physician: How do you arrive at the exact figure?

Psychologist: Each of the so-called subtests — you remembered, for example, a question about a thermometer which belongs in the subtest on informational knowledge — will be scored independently in terms of the number of "correct" answers, or, as in the case of the little designs which you constructed from the picture by using colored blocks of wood, in terms of the accuracy and speed with which you performed that particular task. These so-called raw scores are then changed into uniformly weighted scores (ten points on the Arithmetic Test nets you a weighted score of thirteen, whereas ten points on your little block design, nets you only a weighted score of five). These weighted scores are then added up and it is this figure, combined with the patient's age which will be looked up in a table that will show the already calculated I.Q.

Having insisted on the importance of the I.Q., I will now, in a contrary fashion, reverse my stand and claim that it can also be most misleading, unless properly amplified and explained by the psychologist.

Physician: How so? I thought you just said it was calculated in a routine and invariable fashion by looking up in tables.

Psychologist: That is perfectly true. But, let me demonstrate for you how misleading the simple figure can be. I will take two patients, both of them aged 21. Each of them has a score of 48 for the verbal tests on the Wechsler-Bellevue. This gives them a calculated verbal I.Q. of 101. This, as you will agree, couldn't be more average or "statistically normal." One might expect these two persons to be psychologically identical twins. But now look at the two contrasting diagrams and see how each of them acquired his score. Patient A, for example, really *is* the average, rather mediocre intellectual personality which the I.Q. of 101 might indicate. He does just about equally well or poorly on all the verbal subjects. The scatter, or the deviation between his highest and lowest point on the weighted score is only one. This I.Q. then really represents his type or level of functioning.

But now let us turn to patient B, also 21 and also with his I.Q. of 101, and what a very different picture one finds. You can see how completely erratic his performance is. He does so well in the Memory Test that he scores the maximum obtainable. He does so poorly on the Comprehension Test that he only acquires three points. He has a "scatter," as you will see, of 15 points on the weighted scale. Looking

Chart IV (Part 1)

	Patient A						Patient B				
Equivalent Weighted Score	Information	Comprehension	Digit Span	Arithmetic	Similarities	Equivalent Weighted Score	Information	Comprehension	Digit Span	Arithmetic	Similarities
18	25	20		14	23-24	18	25	20		14	23-24
17	24	19	17	13	21-22	17	24	19	17	13	21-22
16	23	18	16	12	20	16	23	18	16	12	20
15	21-22	17		11	19	15	21-22	17		11	19
14	20	16	15		17-18	14	20	16	15		17-18
13	18-19	15	14	10	16	13	18-19	15	14	10	16
12	17	14		9	15	12	17	14		9	15
11	15-16	12-13	13		13-14	11	15-16	12-13	13		13-14
10	13-14	11	12	8	12	10	13-14	11	12	8	12
9	12	10	11	7	11	9	12	10	11	7	11
8	10-11	9			9-10	8	10-11	9			9-10
7	9	8	10	6	8	7	9	8	10	6	8
6	7-8	7	9	5	7	6	7-8	7	9	5	7
5	6	5-6			5-6	5	6	5-6			5-6
4	4-5	4	8	4	4	4	4-5	4	8	4	4
3	2-3	3	7	3	3	3	2-3	3	7	3	3
2	1	2	6		1-2	2	1	2	6		1-2
1	0	1		2	0	1	0	1		2	0
0		0	5	1		0		0	5	1	

I.Q. 101
Weighted score 48 at 21 years

I.Q. 101
Weighted score 48 at 21 years

at this diagram alone, even though the full significance of the variation of the performance will not be apparent to you, you can at least see that it is a very different type of performance from that given by Patient A and that merely to describe both of them as persons with an I.Q. of 101 is actually a misleading statement.

Chart IV (Part 2)

Patient C

Equivalent Weighted Score	Information	Comprehension	Digit Span	Arithmetic	Similarities
18	25	20		(14)	23-24
17	(24)	(19)	(17)	13	21-22
16	23	18	16	12	20
15	21-22	17		11	19
14	20	16	15		17-18
13	18-19	15	14	10	16
12	17	14		9	15
11	15-16	12-13	13		13-14
10	13-14	11	12	8	12
9	12	10	11	7	11
8	10-11	9			9-10
7	9	8	10	6	8
6	7-8	7	9	5	7
5	6	5-6			5-6
4	4-5	4	8	4	4
3	2-3	3	7	3	(3)
2	1	2	6		1-2
1	0	1		2	0
0	0	0	5	1	

I.Q. 130
Weighted score 72 at 40 years

Patient D

Equivalent Weighted Score	Information	Comprehension	Digit Span	Arithmetic	Similarities
18	25	20		14	23-24
17	24	19	17	13	21-22
16	23	18	16	12	20
15	21-22	17		11	19
14	(20)	(16)	15		(17-18)
13	18-19	15	14	10	16
12	17	14		(9)	15
11	15-16	12-13	13		13-14
10	13-14	11	12	8	12
9	12	10	11	7	11
8	10-11	9			9-10
7	9	8	10	6	8
6	7-8	7	9	5	7
5	6	5-6			5-6
4	4-5	4	8	4	4
3	2-3	3	(7)	3	3
2	1	2	(6)		1-2
1	0	1		2	0
0	0	0	5	1	

I.Q. 115
Weighted score 56 at 55 years

And, while we are on this very important topic, let's take a look at a few more "scattergrams." Not all variations can be justly described as scatter or erraticness. For example, look at Patient C. This is better described as a real defect in one area rather than erraticness of performance. Or, let us say, in all other areas except one, this individual functions extremely well. It so happens that the area where she falls down is that related to Abstract Thinking and the low scores result from the superimposing of personal problems where abstractions were asked for. I'll show you examples of this sort of thing later. This highly personalized thinking made for psychological isolation in an otherwise highly intelligent girl, and indicated the beginning of a rather serious disturbance.

Now contrast this with Patient D who has another type of defect. Again, this cannot be considered real "scatter" for, with the exception of the defect in memory, the rest of the subtest scores cluster close together with a variation of only two points. This individual was tested shortly after shock treatment, which quite frequently produces specific memory defects that show in this way.

Two other types of scatter may be worth contrasting. Again, here are patients with identical I.Q.'s but whose problems as reflected here are entirely different. Patient E, for example, is vulnerable when the tasks she is asked to perform are to repeat a series of numbers or to perform, mentally, arithmetical problems. At this point where she feels she is on the spot, tackling something new, forced to exhibit her efficiency or lack of it, she becomes completely panicky. On the other hand, answering questions about things she has "known all her life," enabling her to draw, from a fund of knowledge, she is able to function extremely well. Contrast this with the diagram of Patient F whose low scores on the Similarities (Abstract Thinking) and on the Comprehension show him to be someone out of touch with the common ways of sensing situations, and to have, like Patient C, a pattern of thinking which deviates from the logical. This patient, however, finds the handling of the

Chart IV (Part 3)

Patient E

Equivalent Weighted Score	Information	Comprehension	Digit Span	Arithmetic	Similarities
18	25	20		14	23-24
17	24	19	17	13	21-22
16	23	18	16	12	20
15	21-22	17		11	19
14	20	16	15		17-18
13	18-19	15	14	10	16
12	17	14		9	15
11	15-16	12-13	13		13-14
10	13-14	11	12	8	12
9	12	10	11	7	11
8	10-11	9			9-10
7	9	8	0	6	8
6	7-8	7	9	5	7
5	6	5-6			5-6
4	4-5	4	8	4	4
3	2-3	3	7	3	3
2	1	2	6		1-2
1	0	1		2	0
0		0	5	1	

I.Q. 113
Weighted score 58 at 29 years

Patient F

Equivalent Weighted Score	Information	Comprehension	Digit Span	Arithmetic	Similarities
18	25	20		14	23-24
17	24	19	17	13	21-22
16	23	18	16	12	20
15	21-22	17		11	19
14	20	16	15		17-18
13	18-19	15	14	10	16
12	17	14		9	15
11	15-16	12-13	13		13-14
10	13-14	11	12	8	12
9	12	10	11	7	11
8	10-11	9			9-10
7	9	8	10	6	8
6	7-8	7	9	5	7
5	6	5			5-6
4	4-5	4	8	4	4
3	2-3	3	7	3	3
2	1	2	6		1-2
1	0	1		2	0
0		0	5	1	

I.Q. 113
Weighted score 58 at 24 years

numerical problems extremely easy; in fact, he flashes back the answers almost as soon as the question is out of the examiner's mouth.

I could multiply such examples almost indefinitely. For every quantitative I.Q., this type of additional information should be given. Not only that, but I feel that it is the psychologist's responsibility at the present stage of exchange of information between our two professions to make quite sure that this type of information is passed on graphically and in an easily understandable fashion.

Physician: I don't see any mention of the little designs I made out of the blocks of wood on the chart we just looked at.

Psychologist: Quite right. The full chart* would be double the size, and would show those subtests which are concerned with *performance* or nonverbal activity. For example, constructing out of little wooden blocks the designs on the printed page or, as you may remember, piecing together, after the manner of a jigsaw puzzle, the man, the face, and the hand, each of which is presented to the subject in pieces. There is also the task of spotting that which has been left out of, or omitted from, a simple drawing.

Taking the whole *verbal* section as a unit and contrasting it with the *performance* section, one can find here evidence of discrepancy or uniformity between these two very general types of activity. As you will readily understand, the person who has great verbal facility but is unable to function when he has to "think" with his hands, or cannot rely on words, is up against different kinds of difficulties from the individual who is competent and at home in relation to things and objects but finds himself baffled and inadequate in the handling of words and ideas.

Physician: It has just occurred to me that if I had had this sort of evidence the other day, in regard to a little chap I saw who was doing so badly in school, I might have been

---

* Full chart on pp. 228, 230.

better able to convince the parents that this boy's mechanical ability should have been encouraged, and the academic career they were planning for him, abandoned. I was called in to see him because of mysterious stomachaches he always had prior to going back to school which proved to be nothing other than the time-honored device of attempting to play hookey. I had the feeling that the parents were trying to force him in a direction he just was not going to go in, but this kind of evidence would have helped me discuss the whole problem with them.

Psychologist: I could give you quite a few instances where minor tragedies have been averted through parental acceptance of a child's actual assets and liabilities on having this type of material explained to them. Not all children resort either consciously or unconsciously to physical symptoms. The other day I saw a girl who had been dismissed from school for cheating and, on examination, she was found to be virtually mentally defective at a verbal level. Psychologists can't perform emergency operations to save lives, but sometimes I have the feeling that to take a child out of a situation where nothing but guilt, confusion, and panic can result, with their damaging and warping effect on the psychological life, is our moral equivalent.

In the time that is left to us now, however, I want to get back to giving you some more information about the individual subtests in the verbal Wechsler-Bellevue, for over and above the material which can be gained from a study of an individual's pattern of performance, that is, whether it is regular or irregular, erratic or uniform — as was demonstrated by the scattergrams — much can be learned from the answers in each subtest which will be scored as "wrong." There is a way of appraising these wrong answers and relating them to other wrong answers which enables us to see certain pressures at work in the individual, pressures which force him into betraying his personal problems, even though he imagines himself to be following the instructions of the test.

Let us take the so-called Similarities Test where the task is to state in which way any two objects are similar or to assess what they have in common. For example, in what way are an orange and a banana alike? In what way are a coat and a dress alike? A dog and a lion? A wagon and a bicycle? And so on. While the correct answer to the first is obviously "fruit," different types of "erroneous" answers may alert the examiner in various ways. A wrong answer expressed in terms of sexual symbolism gives us a clue as to the obsessiveness of the patient's sexual ideas. "*A banana is like a penis; an orange, like a breast.*" A wrong answer expressed in the terms of the similarity of color, on the other hand, reflects the individual's concrete preoccupation with his immediate sensations. For example, they are "*both warm colors.*"

Other wrong answers may reflect the subject's inability to conform to the test instructions as stated, his need, that is, to emphasize the differences rather than what he has been asked for, namely the similarities. "*The one is long, firm, and has more strength; the other is soft and round.*" Or there may be answers which reflect very nicely the individual's essential egocentricity, his incapacity to break away from his own personal life and his tendency to see everything as relating to himself. "*I like fruit. I like a banana better. I like orange juice. It is easier to eat a banana without mess.*" Or again, "*They are alike because they are my favorite fruits.*"

Just to mark all these answers as wrong is to neglect valuable information which the patient gives unwittingly, telling about himself, and while it is obviously unwise to generalize from any one answer alone, a series of such answers will point to unmistakable personality traits.

Let us turn to other types of examples: When the similarity between a coat and a dress is expressed in such a form as, "*The dress is to the pillow what the husk is to the corn,*" we notice, to say the least, a highly unusual way of thinking. Other "wrong" answers of interest to this particular pair of objects may be seen in the following: "*They have a method of fastening which is concealed and they conceal the trunk.*" Here there is obviously a problem in regard to exhibiting the body, so that the more neutral or objective similarity between the coat and the dress, their being clothing, is overlooked in favor of the concealing qualities of clothes.

Answers in regard to the similarity between a dog and a lion are often very revealing when they deviate from the objective appraisal of the similarity, namely, that they are both animals. There is the individual who is determined to display the utmost knowledge at every point regardless of whether or not this knowledge is really relevant. He will, therefore, describe them as "*carnivorous mammals*" with a couple of Latin terms thrown in for good measure. To the individual who is hypersensitive and for whom tactual sensations are an absorbing part of his total experience, a dog and a lion will be equated in terms of their "*soft fur.*"

The individual who is struggling with the problem of his aggressiveness, or conversely with his lack of drive, may estimate the similarity of the dog and the lion in terms of the ferocity and bravery of the one and the tameness of the other. There are people who, still concerned with the infantile problem of eating, will claim that the dog and the lion are alike because *"they both have strong teeth"* or because *"they eat in the same way."* Again, one can have the egocentric individual who sees life in terms of his own small world and immediate possessions, who will claim that his *"particular dog is like a lion."* One can even get the "projection" of extremely personal problems, as, for example, that *"were the dog and lion to be mated they would be mismated"* by a patient who believed his own difficulties to have arisen from the "mismating" of his father and mother.

The question relating to the similarity of praise and punishment often nets us much information, since onto this screen early feelings of guilt and attitudes about how the patient feels himself to have been handled as a child can be easily projected. In particular, the individual with paranoid traits often gives vent to his feelings of being treated with injustice through his reaction to this pair of words. The answers here are frequently loaded with emotion and are consequently very revealing. *"After being praised, one has to be punished."* Or, *"Both praise and punishment hurt alike because they are always unjustified."* Or, *"People praise me only if they wish to punish me."* Or, *"They are both retribution."* Or, *"They are always given unjustly."*

To the question: "What is similar between an egg and a seed," we sometimes find answers which suggest a disturbance in regard to sexual problems. This may take the form of embarrassment and blocking, or these objects may be another excuse for the ventilation of sexual obsession. They are alike because *"they are purely sexual."*

The similarity between the radio and the daily paper is judged objectively to be that of conveying news and information. An extremely self-centered individual, however, will comment: "*They are alike because I very seldom pay attention to either of them.*" It allows the cantankerous individual with a chip on his shoulder against all authority to claim that they are alike because they are "*only used for misinformation,*" or that they are "*merely for propaganda purposes.*"

The similarity between a fly and a tree seems to allow for the projection of some of the more atypical or bizarre ways of thinking. For example, they are alike because, "*They are equally able to take care of themselves, equally able to brush each other off.*" Again, the self-oriented individual can express this by such a statement as, "*I don't like flies; I love trees.*" Sexual obsessions come through, although in a somewhat disguised form, by a statement such as "*They are alike because they both have appendages.*" Some individuals escape the task as such, giving instead some idea which is vaguely associated with both; for example, "*Summer.*"

The similarity between the eye and the ear which would be objectively expressed by their being two of the senses may deviate from this in several directions. To the hypochondriacal patient much concerned over some of his own symptoms, the similarity may be estimated by the statement that "*they are treated by the same specialist,*" or that "*they both give you sleepless nights when they hurt.*" To the individual who is experiencing a certain alienation or a feeling of depersonalization this question may reflect his concern about his relationship to his environment and others. The eye and the ear then become alike because they are "*transmitters of external stimulation.*"

When the individual is asked the similarity between

wood and alcohol, it is almost inevitable that if his problems center around drinking he will be unable to appraise these two words objectively, will block, delay on his reply, and may finally answer, "*Drinking.*" Many people give a wrong, but much more neutral answer, in the statement that the similarity lies in "*wood alcohol.*" This is such a frequent occurrence as to give us very little information about the individuals who give it.

Physician: Would you say then, that, with the exception of a few answers which, though wrong, are given so frequently as to have relatively little personal meaning, every answer that deviates from the objective, neutrally correct answer does so by virtue of the pressure of an individual's personal problems? And that when the pressure is very great, the answer may bear very little relationship to the truth? As I listen to some of these statements, my first reaction is that the individual cannot be serious, but then I realize that his personal problems formulate themselves, so to speak, and seem to utilize these answers as a means of expression.

Psychologist: Exactly. Thus even objective tests become projective ones if given a chance! Now let us consider another subtest which can be projectively evaluated, the so-called Reasoning, Comprehension, and Judgment.

In this test, one gets an idea of the individual's social adjustment and many revealing trends of behavior come to light through the appraisal of the hypothetical situations which are given. For example, take the different answers to the question: What would you do on finding an envelope in the street which is sealed and addressed and has a new stamp?

Physician: Well, that seems quite obvious to me — one would mail it, surely.

Psychologist: Obvious to you, doubtless, but see what a problem it becomes to this disturbed patient who answers, *"If there are people around, I would walk by. I would watch very carefully until there was no one there and then I would go back. If I was high, I might pick the thing up and read it. I would then take it home. I would open the envelope. I would then put it in the typewriter. I would put a different envelope in the typewriter. If there was a return address on it, I would send a letter there saying I don't want to mail this so I will send it back to you."*

Patients with character disorders would *"Look it over very carefully, hold it to the light to see if there were money in it, and if there were, take it."* Or another would *"Read it and then throw it away."* Patients with compulsive indecision describe the experience as being uncertain as to whether to pick it up, mail it, or leave it alone. The markedly withdrawn individual feels no responsibility in regard to picking it up at all and would invariably *"leave it lying there."* Patients with phobias concerning dirt may even reconstruct the question so as to reflect this: *"If it were in the gutter, I would leave it there."*

Another question from this subtest is concerned with the correct thing to do if one is the first person in a theater to discover smoke or fire. In the frankly psychotic individual one gets an answer such as: *"Let the theater burn down and watch it."* There is the exceedingly exhibitionistic individual who would *"go quietly on the stage and hold the audience's attention, keeping them spellbound, and from this outstanding position I would then direct them to march out quietly."* There are answers which run the gamut from:

"Yell 'Fire'," *"Scream 'Fire',"* *"Yell and rush out,"* *"Stand up and shout and rush out,"* to the opposite extreme: *"I would whisper it to the person next to me,"* *"I would sit quite still until someone else noticed it."*

There is a question on this subtest relating to why one should keep away from bad company. This acts like a red rag to a bull to the adolescent who is struggling to assert his independence or to adults in later life who are still busy attempting to justify their revolt against authority. The answer here is almost invariably a tirade against the assumption that there can be such a thing as bad company. Again, individuals whose problems center around their homosexual drives will feel challenged personally by the question and will also repudiate the idea that there is such a thing. The confusion in thinking of one borderline psychotic is seen in his answer: *"Until a proper critical sense is developed, one must keep away from everyone."* An individual with a profound sense of guilt resulting from a recent situational disgrace bursts out with, *"That's a fine question to ask me."* It will be seen here how the personal problem precludes his capacity to judge the question in the abstract.

Guilt, one may say, seeks to find expression regardless of what question is asked. Some persons, for example, are over-burdened by guilt that will seek an outlet at all costs. To the question, therefore, of why are shoes made of leather, they will answer *"because leather can take punishment."* In the same way, there are individuals who are so convinced that people are "putting things over on them" that all established institutions or persons in authority are automatically assumed to be the personifications of evil. Thus, shoes are made of leather because *"the leather industries thereby guarantee that no one else can make a living in the business."* Or, a less violent modification of this, the assumption that all established institutions are arbitrary and the result of the unthinking and stupid people: shoes are made of leather because *"all customs are purely arbitrary."*

The question of what to do on being lost in a forest gives many revealing answers. There is something rather reminiscent of Alice in Wonderland in the answer: *"Consider I was not lost but that those trying to find me were."* Perhaps more than any other question this seems to be an exact replica of the individual's psychological "lostness" which has preceded his coming for therapeutic help and hence psychological examination. There are persons who would *"get panicky."* There are those who would *"be far happier wandering there by myself alone."* There are those who eternally blame the others in the environment: *"I could never be lost because I have such an excellent memory. It would mean that someone had not given me a map."* There are those who would *"sit and wait."* There is the unrealistic individual who cannot face the problem even to the extent of letting the words "lost in a forest" take on their full meaning. Such an individual says: *"Why, of course, I would thumb a ride out of it at once."*

The question as to why persons who are born deaf are unable to speak, frequently catches attitudes toward parents, feelings of injustice in regard to the inheritance of poor physique. For example, *"It happens in the womb; it's because of her syphilis."* Or, *"It's a defect in the mother."* The individual who has repudiated the suggestion that there can be bad company, who has told the examiner flatly that shoes are not made of leather, who has asserted that he would never be lost in a forest, is apt to continue in this vein with a statement that it is *"not true"* that the deaf cannot speak. Persons with strong religious feelings may express them together with guilt and fear of punishment through such an answer as: *"You are born deaf because of an offense in a previous life."*

There is a question in this test in regard to marriage. It is stated as: Why does the state require persons about to be married to get a license? The objective answer here — that it is a matter for the records — is relatively seldom given and attitudes toward marriage are willy-nilly picked up from most persons. Here again we have the group of people who consider that it is only *"a senseless tradition."* We have answers which reflect a fear of lack of order or anarchy resulting from promiscuity. There are answers which harp on the need for *"protection of the woman,"* or, conversely, from male subjects: *"It is what women have put over on us."* It is not hard to see that the answer: *"Because one must have time to think it over,"* comes from a patient whose difficulty centers around a hasty marriage.

Physician: When we were discussing the Rorschach Test you mentioned a patient who spoke of seeing "the timorous sheep hesitantly approaching a hurdle," and you gave from his case history the statement about his indecision in regard to his marriage. Would he have given such an answer?

Psychologist: Yes, he did, and this kind of cross-reference which you mention is most important. Testing with a battery of tests, deriving information from several sources, becomes a matter of finding the dominant themes which appear through the different media. The psychological report is the more valid to my mind, the more varied the evidence it can point to in order to substantiate these central themes.

Physician: How about that test for information? Can wrong answers here be revealing?

Psychologist: There is perhaps less opportunity for interesting deviations on the so-called Information Tests, but some answers or lack of answers point in a specific direction and can be used as corroborative evidence to material that has been derived from other sources.

This test is graded in difficulty through questions as: What is a thermometer? Where is London? How many pints in a quart? to more difficult questions as: What is a habeas corpus? What is ethnology? What is the Apocrypha?

A disturbance may be considered more benign insofar as the easy questions are answered without difficulty while some of the more specialized information is unknown. There is nothing unusual or abnormal, for example, in a high school graduate failing to register an answer to such a question as: What is the Koran? or those previously mentioned at the more difficult end of the scale. On the other hand, we would find it suggestive of severe psychological disturbance if an individual, while answering all these more difficult questions, at the same time did not know how many weeks there were in a year, how many pints in a quart, the date of Washington's birthday, or the capital of Italy. Such an individual's preoccupation with highly intellectual matters would be occurring side by side with complete disregard of some of the facets of normal, everyday living.

As stated before, the deviations from the correct answer here are more often in terms of failures than in projection of personal problems. However, even here we can gather many clues. For example, to the question: What is the height of the *average* American woman? one interesting way in which the individual feels the overpowering presence of a dominating mother looming up from the past or experiences himself dominated by his wife is reflected in the overemphasis of the height of the woman. For example, *"she can be as tall as ten feet,"* or, more realistically, *"five feet eleven"* or *"six feet."*

If an individual has difficulty in defining "what the heart does," it very frequently denotes anxiety attacks in which he has become conscious of a pounding heart or its irregularities. The patient, for example, who defines the working of the heart as *"it does too much"* is clearly someone whose attention has been turned to his own — perhaps pounding — heart rather than considering the question academically.

Our old friend, the individual who is permanently suspicious of the motivations of others, defines the Apocrypha as *"their hypocrisy,"* and again the individual who is burdened by his own sense of guilt finds the habeas corpus to be *"evidence against you."*

Blocking or failure on the easy question: Where does rubber come from? has been shown in the five or six cases in which it occurred to relate to anxiety in female patients in regard to the contraceptives they were using. There are also blockings and failures which may be called topical or seasonal, as, for example, during the war when Tokyo, the capital of Japan, was much in the news. Failure to answer the question: What is the capital of Japan? proved through other associate material to be related to the repression of ideas in connection with rape by Japanese soldiers.

In this particular subtest it is also possible to pick up the individual whose long suit is in his compulsive accuracy and exhaustive knowledge. Such a patient is not satisfied with a simple and correct answer but must dot all the *i*'s and cross all the *t*'s, piling up information regardless of its relevance.

Such an individual, for example, will answer the question: Who invented the airplane? with a historical survey starting with Leonardo da Vinci, proceeding to the Wright Brothers who, he will carefully point out, are erroneously dubbed the inventors. He will answer the question: Who wrote Hamlet? with a discussion of the Bacon controversy.

Some patients will be thrown into quite marked anxiety by questions which relate to numbers. Even though in each instance the number asked for is only "an approximation," the fact that they have to supply a figure somehow makes them feel threatened and "on the spot." Patients who are clearheaded and well informed in almost all other areas may become suddenly overanxious when asked a question as: What is the approximate population of the United States?

Some other overall characteristics are of interest. For example, the (usually hysterical) individual who makes an exaggerated show of his pride having been hurt by being asked the simple informational questions with which this test begins. One patient's voice rose to a shriek of indignation on being asked the question: Where is London? This may be accompanied by such a statement as: *Am I supposed to be back in kindergarten?* Usually the protests are the more vociferous, the more insecure the patient actually feels.

Two remaining subtests in the verbal Wechsler-Bellevue cannot yield quite the same type of psychological clues to the person's makeup as those we have just discussed. These tests for digit memory, on the one hand, and arithmetical ability, on the other, more often reflect ways of responding rather than providing the content of the difficulties.

In particular, the Arithmetic (just like the three questions on the Information in which numbers are involved) may be a direct source of anxiety. The mere mention that the test involves some calculating or simple arithmetical problems is sufficient to throw some persons with neurotic difficulties into a perfect stampede of panic. Moreover, it is quite clear that, on occasion, the anxiety generated by the mere thought of the task is sufficient to disrupt and disorganize the patient's otherwise adequate ability. There can be as much as eight points difference in score on this subtest alone over a period of only two days when one testing interview coincided with a genuine anxiety attack, whereas in the second testing the patient was free of the disturbance which the initial testing had precipitated!

The Arithmetic Test is also an excellent screen to capture the tendency to quit at the first difficulty as opposed to a tenacity which will struggle on despite difficulties. An attitude of "throwing in the sponge" is reflected here better than anywhere else.

Apart from the occasional occurrence of phenomenally good or unusually poor memories, repeating the digits after the examiner — which is the task involved in the Memory Test — does not throw much light on the personality structure. Sometimes it becomes apparent that the individual's inability to repeat the digits is the result of his failure to concentrate while the examiner enunciates them initially because of the pressure of some of his obsessional thoughts which intrude or take right of way over the auditory stimulus of the numbers.

Well, I've talked way over my time, but this may have shown you some of the wealth of material than can accompany the quantitative I.Q.

Physician: Let's see if I can distinguish between the various kinds of information provided. Such a test gives you an I.Q. which would place a patient in terms of his intellectual standing in regard to the total population. It could tell you how erratic or uniform his ways of working in different tasks might be. Then it could tell you of a discrepancy or lack of it between two such general spheres as words and ideas, on the one hand, and nonverbal activities, on the other. Finally, it can give you a wealth of information about internal pressures or unresolved personal problems if you listen to the emotional overtones of the "wrong answers."

Projection Via the Pencil Point

Physician: Is this sheet of paper and pencil laid out in readiness to inveigle me into "projecting my mental organization" by way of doodles?

Psychologist: Not quite doodles — that remains an unexplored area — but in terms of some drawings, yes. I am going to start you off this morning by asking you to draw a person.

Physician: Man or woman?

Psychologist: That's for you to choose.

Physician: Well, I suppose since anything I say in the way of prevarication will be held against me, here goes. (*draws* Fig. III)

Psychologist: Tell me a little about this man.

Fig. III

[124]

Physician: He's a doctor, I suppose, at the hospital; maybe one of my colleagues. He's just off on ward rounds, busy chap, lots on his mind. What are you going to deduce about me from that?

Psychologist: I'm sorry to disappoint you, but I am not going to embark on an analysis of *your* character at the moment. This is an instructional session and it's my job to teach you about the patient's productions. I need your collaboration to get a base line against which you can experience some different types of drawings. I wanted you to get the "feel" of how *you* would respond to such instructions so that I can show you other material in contrast. For instance, what would you feel about this drawing and the patient who drew it?

Physician: Well, as a drawing, it's only a fragment of a man. It's not a complete man, nor a real man.

Psychologist: Fine. Go on. What can you tell about the person who produced this drawing?

Physician: I may be a promising and interested pupil, but I can't say something about a drawing the first time I have ever been exposed to one.

Psychologist: Let me give you a hint as to how to make the transition easier between the drawing itself and the concept of the human being behind it. First, imagine this figure, not as a small line drawing, but blown up to a life-size three-dimensional dummy and taking the surrounding

Fig. IV

paper as the room, place your dummy in it. Now endow this dummy with life. How would he function? What would he do? What would he be *equipped* to do? How would he appear in relation to the room, sitting, standing, lying, walking, too big for it, too small for it, and so on?

Physician: Yes, I see. That is more helpful. If I made a dummy out of this drawing, it would only be half there. It would be a completely helpless and vulnerable creature. It has no legs, no arms, no hands. It couldn't do anything for itself. It's a sort of "basket-case." It's even less than that. Part of the trunk isn't there.

Psychologist: Fine. Now look at this one.

Physician: Why, that's just a figure cut out of cardboard. It's completely flat. It would be hard to endow that with life. There's nothing there. It's so noncommittal.

Psychologist: And, this one.

Fig. V

Fig. VI

Physician: Well, he's at least complete, but he's so tiny. He'd be overshadowed, overpowered. He's lost in that large room. It's almost as if he's apologizing for his very existence.

Psychologist: Now suppose you take the figure of this woman, which incidentally is drawn by the same patient, turn her into another lively puppet and put her in the same room.

Physician: Why, she's so enormous in comparison. He'd be completely dwarfed. She looks cross and angry and he's certainly no match for her.

Fig. VII

Psychologist: That's exactly what his unconscious feels! This is our old friend who, in the Rorschach, expressed certain feelings about marriage in terms of the sheep "timorously approaching the hurdle," who estimated the height of the average American woman as six feet tall in the Wechsler-Bellevue. Interestingly enough he was a man over six feet, himself, so it is clear that this feeling of being overshadowed by the woman is a psychological and not a physical fact.

Physician: Let me see some more women.

Psychologist: Try your hand at this one.

Physician: That's a woman? Why, it's all crossed out. It has only one leg. It's an abstraction, not a human being. Was this meant seriously?

Psychologist: It was meant quite seriously,

Fig. VIII

Fig. IX

but for this patient, much of the life and meaning had gone out of the word "woman." This was drawn by a confused female schizophrenic patient. How do you feel about this one?

Physician: Why the room would be almost filled with the dummy of a head, a beautiful and decorative head, but again only part of a human being. As an animated dummy, it couldn't do much more than blink those beautiful eyes, look pretty and wait for admiration.

Psychologist: How about this one?

Fig. X

Physician: That's clever. How the idea of drudgery can be carried in a few lines!

Psychologist: Yes, it's clever, but sad, too. Life

Fig. XI

as a woman for this gifted but very disturbed girl is epitomized by menial drudgery. This patient bitterly resented
being a girl and wore cowboy clothes whenever possible.
Her main interest in life was horses and during an acute
psychotic episode, she actually fantasied herself as a horse.
When this drawing was made, some time before her breakdown, she combined these two images, herself and a horse,
when asked to draw a man. This type of case, where the
patient has such technical skill and where unconscious fantasies subsequently can be revealed "in the raw," so to
speak, is helpful in understanding graphic productions in
general.

Physician: I don't understand what you mean here at all.
This seems to me to be an excellent drawing constructed by
a perfectly lucid mind. Are you telling me that such a draw-

ing is characteristic of a psychotic patient and that you diagnosed her condition by this test?

Psychologist: I'm glad you stopped me on this because I see that what I have said may have been very misleading. First let me answer you by saying that at the time of the drawing this patient was not psychotic. She was perfectly in touch with reality. Moreover, neither from this drawing, nor, as a matter of fact, from any of the other tests, could it, in my opinion, have been predicted that she would become so acutely disturbed later. I did not mean to say that because she drew a girl-like figure on a horse when asked to draw a man that this *meant* she was psychotic. As a matter of fact quite a few adolescent girls go through a period of including pictures of themselves on horses when asked to draw women and may draw men on horseback when asked to draw men. No, I used this illustration because it seemed to me to show rather nicely that what we draw when asked to portray the human figure relates very intimately to what we believe ourselves to be, even though we may not be in any sense aware of this at the time of the drawing or afterward, for that matter. If a person subsequently becomes psychotic and the barriers are down, so to speak, we have an opportunity to study the fantasies themselves without the camouflages or defenses with which we surround them.

Physician: Well, that at least makes more sense. I was finding it hard to see why the best looking drawing of the lot was going to turn out to be the most seriously disturbed person. Let's go back now for a moment to some of those other drawings. Was I right in what I felt about them? What else would the expert look for and comment on?

Psychologist: You are quite right in your feelings about the drawing in Figure IV. To describe him as a sort of psychological basket-case could hardly be bettered. This was an extremely anxious, functionally inadequate personality. His psychological helplessness was indicated in all the other tests which he took. His psychiatric examination corroborated these findings.

Your statement that Figure V was "completely noncommittal," again came very close to the total appraisal through the battery of tests. This patient was evasive to an unusual degree. He did not wish to have to face up to his own problems and, therefore, hated that anything be known about him. To go back to our old analogy in Chapter II, he made every effort *not* to leave any footprints in the psychological sand.

The patient who drew Figure VI, though actually equipped to function very well, had difficulty in asserting himself, found the task of amassing the more aggressive role in any heterosexual relationship extremely difficult. As I think I said, his acute problem centered around the anxiety he felt as the date of his marriage approached.

Physician: How about the huge and decorative face of the girl which in contrast would seem to fill the whole room?

Psychologist: That was drawn some years ago by a girl who has since turned out to be a highly successful and creative person. At that time, however, she was unusually concerned with herself as a beautiful and charming debutante.

You asked me what details over and above the total impression the expert would look for and what kind of information about the patient he would be seeking. The exhaustiveness of the material which can be extracted from drawings depends, of course, on the amount of experience and the clinical insight of the interpreter. A good illustration of this can be seen in the published work of Machover.* Repeated exposure to many types of drawings, the opportunity to assess these in terms of the clinical findings, results, in some psychologists, in great astuteness and finesse as to the contents of the reports which they can make. There is, as always, an interrelation of the various findings which is of the utmost importance. Here, however, are some of the things one should look for: What type of line is used to produce the drawing? Is it strong and firm or hesitant and wavering? Does it present an unbroken boundary line around the contour of the body as between the individual and his environment or is it more flexible? Then there is the problem of shading: to what extent and where is it used? Excessive shading almost invariably indicates particular anxiety connected with the part of the body that is shaded. Then we would be interested in whether the figure is drawn naked or the type of clothes it is given and with what detail these clothes are handled. There is the question of "transparency" or parts of the body "showing through" the clothing. We have a nice example of this in the sturdy masculine legs with which the lady in Figure VII is endowed. You will see that her skirt is superimposed as an afterthought so that the legs show through. There is also the question of size as you, yourself, pointed out. Very small figures appear almost to be apologizing for themselves. It is also significant which way the figure is looking. Contrast, for example, how your own "man" strides confidently into the picture, whereas the scrub lady shows you no face at all. She has turned her back on the world.

* Machover, Karen: *Personality Projection in the Drawing of the Human Figure.*

Fig. XII

Then there is the question of the omission of certain parts of the body, or, in contrast, overemphasis of some members. One way of handling anxiety arising from the instinctual demands of the body, as such, is simply to conceive of the person as having no body and being a head (intellect) only. Some patients, and these are usually rather seriously disturbed, may conceive of the person as a body without a head, as for example the illustration in Figure XII. This particular patient, tested at a point where he is very close to a psychotic break, struggles to portray the man in terms of wide shoulders and bulging muscular arms, but ends with a broken fragment of the body.

Physician: How about the significance of some of the other parts of the body?

Psychologist: You name them. Which shall it be?

Physician: What do the hands signify?

Psychologist: Let me ask this — what do you do with your hands?

Physician: I work with them. I shake hands. I pick up my child. I caress my wife. I even find I am gesticulating with them now in talking to you!

Psychologist: It would be fair, then, to say that they are, in a sense, the executive members of your psychological equipment. They bring you into direct contact with people and with things. They are active feelers, manipulators, workers. See if you can describe how some of these patients feel about their hands from the way they are drawn. How about this one?

Fig. XIII

Fig. XIV

Physician: He's obviously looking at his hands.

Psychologist: Yes, although I am sure he was not conscious of this when he drew the picture. It happens that this patient's hands are of great concern to him. He is working in a new type of technical laboratory and is afraid that his hands may be damaged.

How about this one?

Physician: Why does it have black gloves on?

Psychologist: This is part of a picture of a motor cop drawn by a delinquent boy. Ostensibly, he justifies the use of the black gloves because the cops wear them. Actually, however, they are an expression of his extreme guilt in regard to his sexual delinquency. Note the position in which the hands are held and the rationalization of the tremendous anxiety that led to blackening them.

There is one other feature of hands that I might mention, and that is when they appear like talons or claws. If a hand actually had sharp points as illustrated here, what would you feel about it?

Fig. XV

Physician: It would appear like a weapon of attack.

Psychologist: Yes. Such features of a drawing are almost invariably confirmed clinically and through the other test findings. They relate to problems of aggression. Sometimes the whole drawing will manifest an overt and outspokenly aggressive attitude, but it is more interesting where the drawing as a whole may keep up the facade of amiability and the claw-like hands may alert us to strong feelings of aggression which the patient is trying to hide.

I'll have to pass on now by exposing you to another test that involves the use of the pencil which you are holding. I want you to think of the most unpleasant thing that comes to your mind.

Physician: Well, I guess that's pretty obvious to most of us these days. The most unpleasant thing . . .

Psychologist: No, don't tell me. Draw it for me.
(*Physician draws* Fig. XVI)

Psychologist: Now you can tell me about it if you like.

Physician: Well, it seems to me that some kind of mass annihilation through a series of atomic blasts would be about the most unpleasant thing to the largest number of people. Can anyone think otherwise at the present time?

Psychologist: You'd be surprised at how many different ideas there are! I've been assessing some five hundred cases recently and find that there are an enormous variety of individual "pet horrors." Some 15 or 20 central trends, however, can be distinguished.

Fig. XVI

Physician: Such as?

Psychologist: Well, I can give you one or two guideposts in case you have the opportunity to observe some of your own patients' performances. I'll start with your own drawing as a point of departure. We might classify this as "Universal Unpleasantness," the greatest distress to the greatest number of persons, or something of that sort. This is the concept most frequently given, you will be pleased to hear, by persons without serious disturbances!

Physician: How would you explain that?

Psychologist: I suppose one could put it this way. The capacity to envisage universal horror presupposes freedom from the most pressing personal problems. You might call it the most neutral, logical, and realistic answer. Deviations from this will mean excessive importance vested in other, more personal concerns.

These deviations could be diagrammatized as going off in different directions from this central theme and the nature of these deviations throws light on some characteristics of the patient's disturbance.

One such group of drawings — one such consistent deviation — occurs in the records of gifted borderline patients; we have called this the "Unpleasant Within." These are highly personal experiences. They belong to one individual alone. The drawings represent, symbolically, a specific person's anxiety, confusion, pain, panic. They are states of consciousness or feelings. But these feelings are drawn *as if* they were objects. Figure XVII, for example, is considered to represent "the loss of selfhood." It is hard for the patient, as he draws these things, to realize that this is not something everyone shares with him in the form that he presents it.

Another quite different deviation from the universal horror is the selection of a small animal — a beetle, bug, mouse, fly — as that which is the most unpleasant thing. These little animals, and they are drawn in all seriousness with great frequency amongst persons with emotional disturbances, strike the neutral observer as strangely trivial. They hardly seem to justify the position of chief importance in the scale of the unpleasant. They *appear* trivial, that is, to those of us who have not projected onto small animals a central core of personal anxiety which makes the animal something frightful and something to be feared. Contrasting this group with the former, we see that the patient here does not recognize fears within himself at all, but unconsciously transfers these fears onto the little animal as if *it* were the troublemaker. Conveːsely, in the case of the symbolic drawings, the patient is only too well aware of his own fear of something within him and it seems to afford him some relief to make of this highly subjective experience an entity or an object. This sharing through momentary objectivity of a devastating subjective experience seems, interestingly enough, to have some therapeutic value. These patients are often relieved once they have completed the drawing.

Physician: Are you concerned here mostly with what is drawn or how it is drawn?

Psychologist: What is drawn is the most important although, of course, there are certain common characteristics which show up whenever a pencil is utilized. Just as in the drawing of the human figures, tentative and faint lines will "belong with" an individual who is extremely hesitant about asserting himself and going on the record.

Physician: How would you use this in an appraisal of a person?

Psychologist: Some broad diagnostic differentiations are possible from it. For example, bizarre ideas and weird types of symbolism, sometimes actual distortions in the thinking

Fig. XVII

process may be caught in the net of this particular test when for some reason they have slipped through other procedures. Or, again, forgotten experiences, some of them quite disturbing, are suddenly triggered and brought to light by this direct question which occurs within the framework of the more indirect procedures. You will notice, for example, that this is the first time you have been asked something directly related to your own life. "What is the most unpleasant thing you can think of?" This is tantamount to asking you to share an unpleasant personal experience.

Physician: I see in this one of the recurring themes of our whole discussions. From one and the same point of departure, from one and the same question, each individual comes up with a response that is not arbitrary, but is part of the pattern of the world he experiences.

Psychologist: Yes. And a world where the most unpleasant thing is a mouse is a world which, for the time being, has lost certain perspectives. But what is important to remember is that for this patient the mouse *is* something frightening. Its frighteningness completely obscures the possibility of this patient's assessing or estimating world-disaster as a catastrophe. One might say that such responses show the direction in which the patient's individual world has become biased. Thus persons without immediate pressing problems are free to assess "unpleasantness" in terms of more universal characteristics.

Physician: I hate to tell you, but I ought to confess at this point that I very nearly drew something quite different, something much less universal and more personal. However, I thought better of it just in time and for once I'll leave you guessing!

[V]

~~~~~~

What's in a Face?

Physician: What are those strange-looking faces?

Psychologist: Suppose I wait to tell you about the test until after you have taken it. Sit down at the table, if you will,
and I'll spread these eight pictures in front of you. I want
you to pick out the two faces that you like best and the two
that you like least. Put the two you like best to your left,
those you like least, to your right.

Physician: Can't say I like any of them very much, but I
suppose that one at the bottom corner isn't too bad. And I
might take as my second choice the last one of the top row.
I dislike most the first one on the top line and the one next
to it is pretty objectionable too. What, you are going to
show me some more of the same kind?

Psychologist: Yes, you'll see 48 pictures in all. I'll give
you six successive series. Each time I want you to do just
the same thing. Pick out the two you like best and the two
you like least.

Physician (making his choice from the successive series

Fig. XVIII

These faces, which closely approximate the Szondi stimulus material, are reproduced here with the permission of Capt. Robert W. Ellis, from whose "experimental" set they have been taken. The artist who drew them is Pfc. R. M. Schilling, Instructional Aids Dept., School of Aviation Medicine, Randolph Field, Texas.

with running comments): This one looks somewhat like my old grandmother. I'll have to pick her. Wherever did you get such a collection of ruffians? Does anybody ever like any of them? Oh, *that's* not a bad face. And, now (*completing the last series*) what is this going to reveal, I should very much like to know. What's the test called and who thought *this* one up?

Psychologist: The test is called the "Szondi" after its originator, a Hungarian psychiatrist. It's a relative newcomer in the field of projective techniques in this country since the material was not available to us during the war. However, Dr. Szondi has worked on it for some forty years and one of his students, Dr. Deri, is teaching it in this country. There is still controversy amongst psychologists as to its validity. Moreover, its basic theoretical explanations are not satisfactory to some people. Nonetheless, it works and can be extraordinarily helpful at times.

Physician: Well, it is not unusual to find a procedure that is helpful diagnostically or some drug which is efficacious therapeutically being used before its action is completely understood. Medicine has many such instances. Brain waves, for example, were put to the task of locating cerebral tumors before there was understanding and agreement as to their exact nature. The Wassermann Test is another instance. It works as a test for syphilis although it is still not understood why. Then there is a drug like digitalis used before science caught up with it, and you will find that some of the conditions which have been shown to be vitamin deficiencies were successfully treated by primitive people who used certain plants. So you see, I'm not one to be against something because it doesn't have an adequate theoretical explanation at the present time.

Psychologist: Good! Then I won't waste time in setting the stage further. The test procedure, as you saw, is simplicity itself. The patient or subject is presented with these 48 photographs in six series, eight at a time. From these he picks the two he likes best and the two he likes least. Now, while each of these 48 photographs is of a different person, each one of the six series contains, as it were, the same ingredients. In each series you were presented with a picture of a homosexual, a sadist, an epileptic, an hysteric, a catatonic, a paranoid, a depressed, and a manic patient.

Physician: What a collection! And what, pray, does liking such a person mean? If I choose a catatonic, do I turn out to be psychotic myself?

Psychologist: No, luckily the rationale is not quite so simple or naïve as that. Let me approach my explanation in a rather general way. You will remember that in one of our earlier discussions, the material from some of the projective techniques was likened to readings taken from the dials in a control room of a hypothetical powerhouse. I drew the analogy that the psychologist was able to gauge the absolute and relative pressures of various tensions within the individual by "reading off" the findings from his tests. This is quite an apt analogy in this instance, for Szondi conceives of the human being as subject to tension in eight specific and measurable areas.

Physician: That doesn't sound too fantastic. Obviously tensions build up in all of us; by looking at your "dials" you could perhaps tell where the maximum pressures are. But how do these facts relate to tensions?

Psychologist: I'll come to that later. We will accept, then, as our first premise, that we are able to measure eight tensions, or, we can ask under how much pressure is an individual with respect to such and such a tension?

Physician: Could you put the question this way: How badly does he *need* something? What "psychologically" is he starving for?

Psychologist: Yes, you could. For there can be emotional as well as vitamin deficiencies. You could go even further and differentiate between an emotional deficiency due to the fact that the actual environment did not contain the ingredients necessary to satisfy these emotional needs or you could say that the patient had a need that was so pathologically strong that, regardless of what opportunities were presented to him in his environment, he would never be satisfied.

Physician: That has a direct physical parallel, too. For instance, the patient with severe hyperthyroidism whose needs for food are so great that he can eat an enormous amount of food and still not satisfy them. But I sidetracked you. What are these needs that you can measure, and, again, please, why these particular faces?

Psychologist: The answers to these two questions are intimately bound up, one with the other, for Szondi envisages each of the eight clinical types which form part of the stimulus material for the test, to be, so to speak, the caricature, the exaggeration or the epitome of the *normal* need which is found in less extreme forms in all human beings. Thus, the second assumption you must make in order to understand this test is that the human face can bear the stamp of some one characteristic at the expense of all others and that, conversely, the observer unconsciously can react to this particular characterization, either by liking it, disliking it, ignoring it, or being ambivalent about it.

Physician: It may sound facetious, but I remember as a small child being told when I looked angry or sulky that if I wasn't careful, the wind might change and that look would get stamped on my face forever.

Psychologist: It's a good illustration, for, while nobody takes that seriously, it shows an acceptance in our culture of the fact that an emotion may be engraved on the face and become a distinguishing or characteristic mark.

Physician: If I liked one of these people then, I would not only like him, but I would also like his "classmates" as they come up in the successive series. This would not mean that I must bear his diagnostic label, but only that I'm in tune with or appreciate a personality trait which he exaggerates, but which might be found in a milder form in an undisturbed person?

Psychologist: Yes, and this brings us to our third set of assumptions. Insofar as you like certain caricatures of normal traits, it means that these are needs within yourself which you are willing to accept, which you "endorse" in your own personality, or tend to live by.

Physician: And, if I dislike them?

Psychologist: As you might expect, it means that you do not accept such a trait as part of your personality. You may repress it in a mild degree or it may be so disturbing to you that you will react violently against it, developing what is called a "reaction formation" in its place. This would be behavior of a type exactly *opposite* to that required by the real need. There's a great difference, however, in the meaning of the Szondi Test where an individual only mildly likes or mildly dislikes a class of faces as opposed to when he dislikes them or likes them so violently that whenever they appear, he chooses them. We speak of these liked or disliked faces when practically all members of the class are chosen as "loaded" reactions.

Physician: You mentioned that it was possible to ignore some types of faces altogether. What would that mean?

Psychologist: If you ignore one of the clinical entities consistently, never picking it either as liking it or disliking it in any of the six series, it is as if these faces have no "pull" on you, one way or the other. You disregard them. They don't stimulate you either in a positive or negative direction. These so-called "open" reactions are considered to relate to those traits which are under no pressure one way or the other. Such lack of pressure could mean one of two things; either that you happen to be someone without that corresponding drive in your makeup or that in the life-situation in which you found yourself, the environment was such that that particular need was constantly satiated. You become interested in any of these faces, one might say, only insofar as there is a surplus tension which is not utilized in the process of living. If a tension actually is lived out, if it is allowed to find its fulfillment in the process of living, then the corresponding face will have no appeal, one way or the other.

Physician: What did you mean about being ambivalent about some of the faces?

Psychologist: That constitutes the fourth possible way of reacting. For instance, in Series I you might like the catatonic face. In Series II, you might again pick it as a positive choice. But in Series III, you might select the catatonic patient as one of your dislike choices. In Series IV you might revert again to a positive choice. In Series V you might ignore this category altogether, but in Series VI you might again dislike this type of face. You would then end up with having chosen five pictures of catatonics. But, clearly, you would be ambivalent about what this class stood for. You would both like and dislike the pictures which caricatured one and the same trait.

Physician: You still haven't told me what these faces caricature. I still don't know what the catatonic stands for.

Psychologist: I know. I am deliberately withholding my explanations so as to utilize your curiosity! At this point, I want to show you how the four types of reactions are recorded and then I will settle down to the main discussion of the character traits. I am going to make a purely hypothetical chart to show you the four different kinds of reactions.

In the first column under "h" (homosexual) is illustrated a "loaded" positive reaction. That is, all the six choices of this particular type of patient were chosen. Each time this clinical entity appeared in the series, it was selected as one of the positive choices. In the second column under "s" (sadist), there is a positive choice which is not loaded. Two of the possible six pictures were selected as those which were liked. Now look under the "e" (epileptics). Nothing has been recorded. This is the so-called "open-type" of reaction. As I said before, at no time has this individual selected the faces in this clinical group as either a positive or negative

	h	s	e	hy	k	p	d	m
Positive choices "Accepted"	X							
	X							
	X							
	X				X			
	X	X			X			
	X	X		X	X			
Negative choices "Repressed"					X	X	X	X
					X		X	X
					X		X	
							X	
							X	
							X	

Chart V. Chart of Szondi Scoring

choice. Another version of the "open-type" of response is recording under the "hy" (hysterics) column when only one choice on the positive and one on the negative is made. This particular type of response is also considered an "open" reaction. Under "k" (catatonics), I have exemplified the ambivalent mode of response. You will see that of the six "k" pictures, all were chosen, but three were liked and three were disliked. Under "p" (paranoids) is yet another example of the "open-type" of reaction, while under "d" (depressed) we have a "loaded" negative choice. That is, all the possible pictures in this group have been chosen as being amongst those disliked most. Under "m" (manic) is another example of negative choice where only two of the possible six pictures were selected, but in each case they were disliked. Now, if you will add up the totals you will find that this hypothetical individual has chosen his 12 positive choices and his 12 negative choices.

Physician: Surely this is an extremely simple test to administer and score.

Psychologist: Its simplicity and rapidity gives it a distinct advantage over others; one of these is the possibility of having the test administered prior to a daily therapeutic session by an assistant in the therapist's office. Then information derived from the test can run parallel to material which comes to light in the therapeutic hour. One can, in this way, satisfy experimental conditions, for the two sources of material can be kept quite distinct and conclusions drawn from each independently until such time as it seems pertinent to see how they interact.

Physician: Can the test be repeated as often as that?

Psychologist: Not only can it be repeated, but it should be, for unlike the other projective techniques, the standard administration of the Szondi Test requires that it be given several, preferably as many as eight or ten, times to each patient during approximately the same number of days. That is, it is not a "single" test profile that is sought, but a series of such profiles, for in this test the *changes between performances* are part of the material that is analyzed. We are interested, for example, in whether a "loaded" reaction stays loaded over a period of time. For, clearly, permanent or prolonged tension in any one area is a very different condition from a momentary one.

Physician: Is the test invalid if you only give it once?

Psychologist: Not invalid — just less complete. Perhaps one could put it this way: When it is used as a single instrument it must be repeated. When it is used as one of several tests the additional information which you get from a single presentation is very much worthwhile.

Physician: It seems to me that by now you must have brought me to the point where I can be let in on the rationale behind the use of these particular faces.

Psychologist: I am not deliberately trying to hold out on you. But the fact is that I have discovered after long experience that it is better not to rush into these explanations too early in the game. They seem improbable and farfetched unless one works up to them in a more general discussion.

We start out then with four main tension systems, each of which has two component parts. These tension systems are called "vectors." In the first, the Sexual Vector, are two components which have as their exaggerated expression, on the one hand, pictures of homosexuals; on the other hand, pictures of sadists. The reason for this is that sexuality as conceived by Szondi and measured by the test contains two distinct but interrelated facets; basically, a passive and an active component. Under the passive, "feminine," or receptive aspect of sexuality come all the tender emotions related to being loved, being cared for, being the recipient of another's care and affection. The active or "masculine" component of sexuality epitomizes the need for sexual aggression, for physical contact with the love object. It relates to the need to be the initiator in love relationships and to the direct expression of sexuality through physical means. Outside the sphere of sexuality proper, acceptance of this drive will mean energetic action, interest in physical activity.

Physician: And do these normal ingredients of sexuality have to be represented by two deviates, a sadist and a homosexual? Why couldn't you show the faces of sexually normal individuals?

Psychologist: You are forgetting that the basic assumption of this test is that the so-called "normal" need is represented by exaggerated distortions of it. It is probably inherent in the nature of things that balance or lack of tension will not leave a characteristic mark for that need.

Physician: All right, I will drop the pursuit of that particular argument. It would follow, however, from what you say that to accept in oneself the two normal ingredients of sexuality would indicate normal functioning.

Psychologist: In one sense, yes. But even there, I would have to hedge a little. You could say with certainty that if the individual gave plus (accepting) scores in these two components of the Sexual Vector, he or she was not suffering from a neurosis based on a repression of sexual drive. But, depending on the rest of the personality as shown by the other scores, his acceptance of sexuality could mean a normal adult sexual adjustment or it could also mean a need for the direct expression of sexuality at all costs, even if it resulted in inappropriate behavior. For example, plus scores in the Sexual Vector may be given by psychotics who will masturbate in the presence of others. Such scores may reflect promiscuity or the inability to sublimate sexual drives.

Heavy "loading" of both Sexual Vectors almost always indicates sexual disturbance. One cannot say in the Szondi that it is "impossible to have too much of a good thing," for too much of *anything* is a sign of disturbance.

Physician: A modern version of Aristotle's Golden Rule for the Happy Mean.

Psychologist: Yes. The projective techniques, by and large, are a living embodiment of this maxim and the Szondi, more than any of them, seems to depend on it.

Physician: Supposing someone rejects these needs and dislikes both these types of faces?

Psychologist: The meaning of this would again depend on how violent the disliking was. If both components were "loaded" in a negative direction, we would expect a disturbance reflecting a denial or repression of sexuality which would leave its mark on the personality as a whole. On the other hand, a mild degree of disliking can correlate with successful sublimation of sexual impulses into other channels.

Physician: Are there other possibilities over and above accepting or rejecting these impulses?

Psychologist: Yes, there are 16 possible ways in which these two components can be related to each other, for you will remember, not only is there the possibility of showing acceptance or rejection, but either or both can be under no tension, and either or both can show the type of tension resulting from ambivalence, uncertainty, in regard to accepting or rejecting them. But this is where we get into the specialist's province, whereas the goal I set myself in regard to this test is to bring you to a point where the psychologist's report is neither arbitrary nor meaningless and where a chart showing "loaded" reactions, for instance, can tell you a significant story.

Physician: That's fair enough; let's get on to the next, what did you call it, vector?

Psychologist: The next vector relates to the way, or shall I say the rhythm or pattern, of how emotions are handled and expressed. The name which Szondi ascribes to it is the Paroxysmal Vector. It has two component parts represented by pictures of epileptics, on the one hand, and pictures of hysterics, on the other.

Physician: Well, here I must confess I am completely at sea. Homosexuals and sadists in some way relate to the province of sexuality, I am willing to admit. But what these two clinical groups have in common, or why they should epitomize characteristic ways of expressing emotion is hard to see.

Psychologist: Let's approach it in a little different way. I think we all know people whose emotional patterns seem to take the form of long stretches of controlled and considerate behavior, broken by some sudden, explosive emotional outburst. At the other extreme, one might say, we have acquaintances who are somewhat overemotional all the time, but who never indulge in excessive outbursts. Metaphorically, one might say of the latter type that since water is spilling over the dam all the time, the dam is never likely to burst, whereas for the first type, there will be periodically a breakdown of the structure which is holding the reservoir of emotions in check. For Szondi, the epileptic patient, with periodic outbursts of violent activity, seems to provide the epitome of this type of control, that is, behavior broken by sudden devastating outbursts. Whereas the hysterical patient displays a continual exaggeration of his inner experiences in his overt behavior.

Physician: Well, that's beginning to make sense. What would it mean, however, if I liked the epileptic faces?

Psychologist: The pictures of the epileptics who form the stimulus material in this test were all taken at the period between seizures when, according to Szondi, the epileptic, himself, would be compulsively concerned with restraining his own aggressive impulses, that is, would experience pressure toward behaving in an acceptable way. Liking these faces amounts to saying, "I endorse, I approve of not exploding emotionally, of holding myself in check, of being considerate of others." On the other hand, when many of these faces are picked as negative choices, disliked, an emotional outburst of some kind (or its physiological concomitant as an epileptic seizure in the epileptic patient) can be safely predicted.

Physician: You mean that epileptics themselves make different selections in this test at different stages in their cycles?

Psychologist: Yes, Szondi's findings show very clearly that "loaded" negative choices precede an attack and that immediately after an attack, this area is tensionless, drained, or as I have described it before, exemplified by "open" reactions.

Physician: You're not trying to tell me that an epileptic attack is just a burst of anger, are you?

Psychologist: As a matter of fact, I am not, although poetically, I suppose you could speak of the body's rage and frustration as being expressed in an attack. Moreover, the role of emotions in precipitating attacks is far from sufficiently studied or understood. What I am trying to point out here, however, is the similarity in the "pattern" in a burst of anger in an otherwise controlled person, and the burst of disorganized activity that disrupts the life of the otherwise well-controlled epileptic patient. In order to see this striking similarity, and to understand the use of these faces in the test as showing a certain type of control and loss of it, it is not necessary to see the attack *as* a burst of anger.

Physician: That's interesting. I'd like to think about it anyway. Now, if I like the hysterics, I am endorsing what?

Psychologist: That it is acceptable to show emotions, that exhibitionistic needs are tolerated, that the display of emotion is more important than the inner psychological experience itself. A combination of these two factors allows for a very wide description of patterns of emotional behavior varying from one extreme of the most controlled, careful, and undemonstrative person possible, to a completely impulsive and exhibitionistic individual.

Physician: Let's see if I can now figure out for myself what scores such people would have. A very controlled individual would have to like the epileptic faces. He would have to have, what do you call it, a plus "e" score because he would have set up barriers against allowing himself to blow off explosively. At the same time, he would not tolerate in himself any exhibitionistic display, so that he would have to dislike the faces of the hysterics. And, having got that far, I would suppose that your impulsive exhibitionistic individual would have to show exactly the reverse scores. He would dislike the pattern of careful control and he would feel in harmony with those persons who wore their hearts on their sleeves.

That's four of the eight tensions accounted for. Now, what comes next?

Psychologist: The next vector, spoken of sometimes as the Ego Vector, has as its two components, pictures of catatonic and paranoid patients. These clinical groups reflect, on the one hand (catatonic), a tendency on the part of the person to contract and wall himself off from others, and, on the other (paranoid), the need to expand, dilate, and merge with others. The catatonic has pushed this necessary walling off process to such an extreme that he can completely disregard others and live in a world of his own. The paranoid, on the other hand, has pushed the concept of "merging" to such an extreme that he has broken down the barriers between himself and others. He does not know which are the boundaries that separate him from the rest of the world. Thus he thinks that his own ideas are actually in the minds of others. They appear to come from them. However, as you know by now, these extremes, these pathological forms of behavior, have nothing to do with the normal needs which accepting or rejecting these faces in moderate amounts signifies.

Physician: In what way may I be legitimately paranoid? What does it show if I like the paranoid faces?

Psychologist: You would accept consciously the need to be emotionally driven beyond yourself, to become involved in or involved with other things or persons and by so doing extend your own frontiers and boundaries.

Physician: And, by disliking the faces?

Psychologist: By disliking the faces, particularly if the reaction was "loaded," you would not have denied this need to go beyond yourself, but you would, as it were, be acting blindly without the intellectual realization that you were thus involved. This particular type of unconscious emotional projection, this intense and abandoned "living into things," is found, paradoxically enough, amongst severely disturbed psychotics and gifted artistic creators. Which brings me back to my central theme that isolated reactions mean very little.

Physician: Or it might mean that "genius is akin to madness!"

Psychologist: A fascinating theme on which, incidentally, the projectives have quite a lot to say. But that is another story.

Physician: How about the catatonics?

Psychologist: The normal need of which the catatonics' isolation is the extreme may be likened to that part of the self which organizes experiences, keeps things in order, does not allow the expanding impulses to run riot, so that the core of the self is depleted. It is the part of the self that wants to be sure that the person's *own* house is kept in order and that there are enough supplies in the closets to guarantee his security. Thus, when there are relatively many catatonic choices, the chance of the individual's overextending himself, of becoming involved passionately in some personal cause, is greatly lessened. Conversely, when the catatonic choices are few, the expanding part of the personality is free to abandon itself to, or become carried away by, external projects.

Physician: Here, again, if there are 16 possible ways in which these interrelated tensions can be expressed, I can see that you can epitomize many different types of personalities, varying from the individual who lives within his ivory tower and concentrates on his own interests, to someone who will dedicate himself with abandon to another person or a cause with complete disregard of the need to harbor his own resources.

You have one more vector to discuss, haven't you? You mentioned depressed and manic patients. How do they fit into the scheme of things?

Psychologist: They both represent aspects of what we call the Contact Vector, since the exaggerated tensions reflected in these faces relate to the need which we have in regard to other persons, other things, to the way we make contact with the world around us. With what sort of attitude, we might ask, do we approach other persons, our physical possessions, both of which are "objects" other than ourselves?

The theoretical justification of the use of these faces in this way is both complex and controversial, so this time I am going to start on an empirical level and talk about some of the constant test findings in this connection. For instance, persons who dislike the manic faces are, without exception, unhappy and pessimistic in their outlook. They are resigned and sad. It is as if they have renounced their right to enjoy others. They expect no pleasurable experience from them. On the other hand, persons who like the manic faces (in moderation) are those who are socially well-adjusted, at least in the sense that they are able to enjoy interpersonal relations. Those who like the manic faces excessively are usually experiencing acute anxiety. They crave continual emotional support from others, for without it they feel panicky and insecure.

Physician: Those would be the persons then with "loaded" "m" reactions? What if one is ambivalent in regard to this need?

Psychologist: Why don't you figure it out?

Physician: I suppose they would be torn between wanting to get satisfaction from others and, perhaps because of some unfortunate interpersonal relationships in the past, they would also have the feeling that close contacts are not pleasurable and should, therefore, be avoided. They would, I should think, be in a state of tension and conflict, uncertain as to what to aim for in friendship and love.

Psychologist: Yes, such people are usually more acutely unhappy than those who have attempted the solution of interpersonal relationships by giving up hope that they can be found to be satisfactory.

Physician: Is it possible to have no tension in this area?

Psychologist: Yes. Lack of all conflict, or a constant "open" reaction would mean not so much that the individual was endlessly satisfied in human relationships as that he was taking out his satisfaction in substitute ways, perhaps by relying on more direct expression of his "oral" needs.

Physician: That, I don't understand.

Psychologist: This is where we get tied up with a theory I had hoped to avoid, but it would run something like this. We have to make the hypothesis that the manic, as a baby, was not satisfied with what he derived from the first world outside himself that he ever knew, namely, the mother's breast. He was, in short, a feeding problem who, as a result of this original and basic frustration, frenziedly tries, throughout the rest of his life, to make up for it. He wants to, metaphorically, "suck" from the world an endless source of satisfaction to make up for the original deficit. During the hypomanic phase he envisages the world and other people as a place of heightened and perpetual excitement, a place from which excessive enjoyment can be drawn. Photographs of the manic patients which are used in the test are taken during this period and, therefore, epitomize an exaggerated delight in relation to the expectation of what can come from others.

Physician: Well, I see what you mean about it being controversial and complex. But I suppose it might work for all that. Now, how about those depressed patients?

Psychologist: While the manics were feeding problems, the depressed patients, to use the same vernacular, had a stormy time over toilet training. In consequence, and you may know the analytic theory in regard to this, they may be unduly threatened by the idea that they may lose something that belongs to them. Security, it seems, lies in possession. Thus, the exaggerated expressions on the depressed patients' faces epitomize a worrying anxiety lest it may not be possible to get things, or that things may be taken away from them.

Physician: So, liking them would mean . . .

Psychologist: Endorsing in oneself the characteristics which go with acquiring new possessions, new persons and new interpersonal relationships, enjoyment in the doing of things with objects, in controlling them.

Physician: And disliking?

Psychologist: Security here seems to lie in remaining attached to a few basic objects or persons, a conservative attitude, a loyalty at all costs, even if unrealistic. While the ambivalent reaction, as always, signifies a conflict, "Shall I seek out new things or stick to the old?"

Physician: And the "open" reaction, the man without tension?

Psychologist: Just that. He is not glued to any particular object, either old or new. He has the advantage of being free from hampering attachments with the vulnerability that goes with it. He might, in the words of the poet have "freedom, but freedom's isolation and loneliness," as well.

Physician: It is hard to assimilate all this, but I comfort myself that I don't have to remember the details in such a way as to draw any conclusions. I will say this for it, however, it makes more sense than seemed possible when we started out and probably it will grow on me as some of the other tests have.

[VI]

~~~~~~

Psychological Barometers

Physician: I see you are ready to go on to another test today, but I was wondering whether we could spend a further session on those faces. I won't say I didn't understand what you told me yesterday, but if you could do something comparable to the second session we had when considering the Rorschach Test, it might help me. Those charts you showed then of the different "psychological worlds" gave me something to hang on to and started me off with a frame of reference.

Psychologist: By all means. All we'll have to do is to go through some case histories and look at these "psychological barometers" drawn on the Szondi charts at the same time. Let's move over to my desk where I can reach my files more easily.

Physician: I brought along that little chart that you made out for me yesterday (*see* Chart V), showing what the various types of "positive" and "negative," "loaded," "ambivalent" and "open" responses looked like. I can use that to refer to. But the trouble is that I don't seem to be able to remember what these clinical characters really stand for!

Psychologist: We can remedy that very easily, for you are not the only one who has had trouble with this. In fact, I had to devise a different type of chart the other day for a group of students to cover just this point. So, for the time being, forget all about the homosexuals, the sadists, and the other members of the clinical team. For in this chart I have expressed the *normal* needs instead of the deviants. I shan't put in all the scores in every case, but only those which are particularly relevant to understanding the dynamics.

Here, for example, is a young man in the army, constantly being sent up for disciplinary action. (Chart VI)

His "loaded" scores are very much what you would expect, I think. Look at the pressure in the aggression column. See how he handles his emotions. A direct and uncontrolled display. And, look at his attitude toward people. He expects nothing from them emotionally and so has no restraining influences arising from the need to get on well with others.

Now, let's contrast this with another man who is having difficulty in adjusting in the army and has been referred for psychiatric appraisal. Some question has arisen as to whether or not this man is schizophrenic. From the battery of tests, it transpired that there probably was a latent schizophrenic process, but without going into the diagnosis at this point, let's see what these pressures tell in themselves. (Chart VII)

Here is someone who also doesn't expect others to give him any emotional support, but he is behaving very differently from the patient whose record we just looked at. He is really saying, "Others are so unnecessary, they hardly exist." The pressures here relate to "not wanting to be loved," on the one hand, and a desire to live in his own highly individualized world, on the other. This patient is

	SEXUAL		PAROXYSMAL		EGO		CONTACT	
	h	s	e	hy	k	p	d	m
	I need to be loved	I need to love and act aggressively	I need to control my emotions	I need to show my emotions	I need to keep my individuality — to be apart	I need to merge into others — to expand	I am pressed to search for new objects (restlessness)	I need to enjoy and be sustained by people
		X X X X X	X X X X X	X X				X X X
	I don't want to be loved tenderly	I want to be submissive. I don't want to be aggressive	I want to let my anger out	I need to hide my emotions	I need to deny my individuality	I am unaware of my need to expand — and I do so without insight	I am pressed to stick to one object (loyalty)	I don't expect pleasure from people

Chart VI. The Anti-Social Character in the Army (Only particularly relevant scores given; see p. 163)

Chart VII. The 'Hermit' in the Army (Only particularly relevant scores given; see p. 163)

	SEXUAL		PAROXYSMAL		EGO		CONTACT	
	h	s	e	hy	k	p	d	m
Positive pole	I need to be loved — **X X X X**	I need to love and act aggressively	I need to control my emotions	I need to show my emotions	I need to keep my individuality — to be apart — **X X X**	I need to merge into others — to expand	I am pressed to search for new objects (restlessness)	I need to enjoy and be sustained by people
Negative pole	I don't want to be loved tenderly	I want to be submissive. I don't want to be aggressive	I want to let my anger out	I need to hide my emotions	I need to deny my individuality	I am unaware of my individuality — my need to expand — and I do so without insight	I am pressed to stick to one object (loyalty)	I don't expect pleasure from people — **X X X**

walling himself off, attempting to be oblivious of others, and by so doing is living a life which in one sense is relatively free from conflicts and distress, but, in another sense, is flying in the face of reality. He might be a successful hermit, but as a soldier, he is having trouble.

Physician: You mentioned earlier that one of the important features about this test is the fact that it picks up changes in behavior. Do you have some cases where one can see a longitudinal section as well as a cross section of living?

Psychologist: Yes, indeed. Here is an example of a man whom I was able to follow for nearly two years. I first tested him at the time when he was about to embark on psychotherapy and I have seen him emerge successfully from this treatment. The four "slices of life" shown here are interesting. (Chart VIII, VIII A, B, C)

This is a gifted commercial artist who was around thirty when he was first seen. He was being shamelessly exploited by the firm for which he worked, a fact which he realized but which he was unable to do anything about. He was neither able to assert himself and ask for more money, nor get out and find a better job. He was, to speak, frozen or immobilized in this hopelessly unsatisfactory situation. Also, he had already had two unhappy marriages, emerging from the second considerably battered emotionally by the experience. The Szondi portrays the situation very clearly. In regard to his job, what we might call his negative aggression, his inability to assert himself, prevents him from getting his rightful dues professionally. (Minus "s.") Added to this, he is so anxious for people to like him and so much in need of helpful and sustaining figures around him that he does

SEXUAL		PAROXYSMAL		EGO		CONTACT	
h	**s**	**e**	**hy**	**k**	**p**	**d**	**m**
I need to be loved	I need to love and act aggressively	I need to control my emotions	I want to let my anger out	I need to keep my individuality — to be apart	I need to deny my individuality	I am pressed to search for new objects and be sustained by people (restlessness)	I need to enjoy and be sustained by people
X X X X					X X X		X X X X
I don't want to be loved tenderly	I want to be submissive. I don't want to be aggressive	I need to show my emotions	I need to hide my emotions	I need to merge into others — to expand	I am unaware of my need to expand — and I do so without insight	I am pressed to stick to one object (loyalty)	I don't expect pleasure from people
	X X X X						

Chart VIII. The Gifted Commercial Artist (Only particularly relevant scores given; see p. 163) not dare to do anything that may cause him to be looked on with disapproval. (Minus "k" and strong plus "m.") But, at the same time, he is demanding in his marriage relationship that he assume completely the passive roll. He needs to be loved exorbitantly.

If we look at the two key scores a few months later, after he has been launched in therapy, we find something which is at first sight surprising, namely, that his condition seems to have worsened. (A)

He seems to be *more* dependent and *more* submissive. There is a rise in the "h" scores, greater negative pressure in "s." This is understandable, however, when one realizes that the first stage in many therapeutic relationships is a period when the patient abandons himself, so to speak, to the help and protection of the therapist. Finding someone apparently strong on whom he can rely, who will help him, his dependent and submissive traits almost run riot.

Tested again eight months after the start of therapy, we find that these needs are now no longer under extreme tension, that they have assumed much more normal proportions. Their interrelationship is still one in which the man assumes somewhat of a passive role, but not to the extent that we would expect it to disrupt interpersonal relationships. (B)

At this point, the patient was able to disentangle himself from the job in which he was being exploited and consider the possibilities of working on his own.

When, eighteen months after the start of therapy, we next take our depth sounding, we find another change and, in this patient, a change which is definitely for the good. (C)

Not only is he merely not so submissive as he was before, but he is able to accept his own aggressiveness and strike out

Chart VIII A.

SEXUAL	
h I need to be loved	**s** I need to love and act aggressively
X X X X X	
	X X X X X
I don't want to be loved tenderly	I want to be submissive. I don't want to be aggressive

Chart VIII A.
Artist's Scores a Few Months Later

Chart VIII B.

SEXUAL	
h I need to be loved	**s** I need to love and act aggressively
X X	
	X X
I don't want to be loved tenderly	I want to be submissive. I don't want to be aggressive

Chart VIII B.
Artist's Scores Eight Months Later

Chart VIII C.

SEXUAL	
h I need to be loved	**s** I need to love and act aggressively
X X	X X
I don't want to be loved tenderly	I want to be submissive. I don't want to be aggressive

Chart VIII C.
Artist's Scores Eighteen Months Later

legitimately for himself in a field where he was more than competent to compete with the best. At this same time he married again.

Physician: And the story should end, "... and is now living happily ever after!" But what a complicated business living is. How do we ever steer a safe course between too much and too little? Too much aggression and you're in trouble with the law; too little and you're stuck in an underpaid job. And such fundamental differences of behavior being carried by, and reflecting themselves in, just the number of sadistic faces that are liked or disliked! You were quite right to introduce me to this test by gradual steps. Otherwise I would have reiterated my original argument that momentous conclusions are being drawn from such tiny clues. By the way, what is my Szondi "profile" like? Where are my test scores?

Psychologist: You know that it's strictly against the dictates of my professional conscience to turn over test results to a patient! However, since you have that little chart in your hand, I see no reason why you shouldn't plot the findings for yourself. You can let me know sometime whether your conscious and unconscious appraisals of yourself agree, one with the other!

[VII]

▰▰▰▰▰▰▰▰▰▰▰▰▰▰▰▰▰▰▰▰▰▰▰▰▰▰▰▰▰▰▰

The Self in Sentences

Physician: I think you said last time that we were almost at an end of our experimental sessions. You still have some new material for me?

Psychologist: Yes, I'd like to expose you to one other experience, one other method of projection. Your task is again a very simple one. I want you to complete a sentence which I shall leave unfinished, hanging in midair.

Physician: Such as?

Psychologist: Few children fear . . .

Physician: Few children fear *cancer*.

Psychologist: What made you say that?

Physician: Well, it seems to me quite obvious. A child simply doesn't know about cancer, so how can he be afraid of it? Whereas the physician who has seen patients in the terminal stages must, of necessity, be aware of its painful possibilities. Such an answer clearly has nothing to do with me. It's so obvious, I should think everybody would say it.

Psychologist: Would you imply then that there are no other painful forms of death?

Physician: Of course, there are! Suffocation, heart attack, or death from peritonitis.

Psychologist: But you said, "Few children fear *cancer*." You made a selection; you didn't say "Few children fear . . . *any form of painful death*."

Physician: Now that's very odd. I just remembered as a very small child hearing my father discuss the details of his mother's death and being terrified by the description and having been haunted by the word "cancer" for sometime after that. That's very strange; the whole thing comes back to me quite suddenly and I had completely forgotten all about it.

Psychologist: That's interesting. It almost looks as if the sentence, "Few children fear . . ." gave you an opportunity to recapture that memory. And you see what has happened? For, without knowing it, you have told me something of your early fears even though, intellectually, you could prove that a child realistically cannot know enough about cancer to be afraid of it in the way that a physician is, shall we say, entitled to be. The thing which you have, by your answer, exonerated the child from fearing is something which you, as a child, feared yourself, and since the child is father to the man, probably still have some residual anxiety about.

Physician: Okay, you win. There is more of the personal than the academic in that statement, I admit.

Psychologist: I know it is frequently exasperating to discover in the neutral and the harmless something that is personally tinged. But, it isn't really "losing" or the psychologist "winning." I should rather say that the psychologist can "win" with the help of his instruments only insofar as he can make them yield pertinent and significant information about the patient he is examining. The projective techniques are valuable in the hands of the psychologist to the extent that they show characteristic facets of the individual's continuous struggle to adapt and adjust to life situations. Too much weight attached to a single answer and the whole complexion of the personality being assessed may change. A psychologist "loses" when he becomes irrelevant to the main issue at hand. This brings me to my next point. The answer to any single sentence cannot tell the whole story. It becomes characteristic of the patient's way of behaving. Let me illustrate this for you in terms of some more of your own answers. How about, Children are usually certain that . . . ?

Physician: There is a Santa Claus.

Psychologist: There is hardly any . . .

Physician: Thing as satisfactory as shooting a round in par.

Psychologist: Worse than being lonely is . . .

Physician: Being stuck with boring company.

Psychologist: A large crowd . . .

Physician: Watches the Army-Navy game.

Psychologist: If people only knew how much . . .

Physician: They don't know, they'd be less hasty to generalize.

Psychologist: That'll do fine. Now compare your answers with these: "Children are usually certain that . . . *they will get well.*" "There is hardly any . . . *thing worse than being sick.*" "Worse than being lonely . . . *is being an invalid.*" "A large crowd . . . *gathered at my bedside.*" "If people only knew how much . . . *I suffer, they would not criticize me.*"

Physician: Well, he's certainly got a one-track mind!

Psychologist: That's exactly the impression I wished to convey, for you will see that all these "opportunities" for projection are utilized by this patient only to harp on the idea of illness. "Few children fear cancer," therefore, would mean something very different in the total personality of this patient from what it did in your case.

Physician: What would you make of my answer. "Children are usually certain there is a Santa Claus?"

Psychologist: Don't you know it is always the psychologist's privilege to reverse the question and say, "What do *you* make of it?

Physician: Well, it seems to me it might mean I was a very lucky child and got many of the things I wanted so that I faced life with the assumption that good things came "out of the blue." Or, perhaps if I'd been just the opposite, it would be a sort of "whistling in the dark," wishing I could believe in Santa Claus and finding it impossible.

Psychologist: Either of those interpretations might be correct and we would have to see how things unfolded or developed throughout the rest of the sentences. It would be safe to say, however, that you were concerned with giving or getting presents in a way that was a little tinged with magic. Using this answer of yours as a base line, you might compare it with those answers which are concerned primarily with receiving affection, specifically an emotionally starved person can reply, "Children are usually certain that . . . *their mothers love them.*" Some people who also have been denied early affection may complete the sentence with "*that they will get food.*"

Physician: I begin to get the feel of the different directions in which these answers can go and if you have many such sentences, each one with numerous possibilities, you must end up with an extremely complex network or web woven by the person in terms of his satisfactions and frustrations, fears and longings. By the way, how many sentences are there in this test?

Psychologist: There are around seventy in the particular test which, incidentally, I should introduce to you by name. It is known as the Miale-Holsopple Sentence Completion Test. There are several Sentence Completion tests available, but this one utilizes an indirect approach that is much more closely in line with the ideas inherent in the projective techniques which we have already discussed. You will notice, for instance, that none of the sentences here relates directly to the person concerned. It is not "As a child I feared . . .," nor "My father should learn that . . .," but the more neutral, "Few children fear . . .," "Fathers should learn that . . ."

But to go back to what you were saying before, that is where the expert comes in. Extraordinarily detailed and precise estimates of the individual are possible when the experienced psychologist has seen hundreds of completions to each of these sentences and has developed a sensitivity for their interrelatedness. As I have said many times, I am not here to teach you the detailed interpretations or to turn you into a psychologist any more than you could complete my medical education in the course of a few weeks. This is a field, where, in my opinion, a little knowledge *need not be a dangerous thing.* It would become so only if you usurped the psychologist's role. A little knowledge should be an enlightening thing insofar as you may be freed from hampering skepticism and are increasingly able to understand and perhaps discuss the psychologist's findings with him.

Physician: Let's have some more examples. How would you tie this test in with your other ones?

Psychologist: In many cases I would use it to accentuate certain central themes which had appeared in the other media. I would use it to try to pick up specific content when a more generalized disturbance had been indicated by the tests which are more concerned with the structure of the personality. For example, let me read you a series of answers given by a twenty-one-year-old girl. In this instance I was working "blind" and the purpose of the examination was for "an independent appraisal of the depth and severity of the patient's disturbance." From the other test findings I had already established good intelligence. I had ruled out a psychosis, for this patient's contact with reality was excellent, but had found her to be in an emotional turmoil. These sentences fill in some important gaps in the understanding of her difficulty.

To the sentence, "No one can repair the damage caused by . . .," she adds, "*a broken heart.*" When confronted with "Worse than being lonely is . . .," she completes it with, "*having unrequited love.*" When given "Nothing is harder to stop than . . .," she replies, "*your feelings toward someone.*" To, "There is hardly any . . .," she adds, "*way to make a person love you if they don't.*"

Apparently then, this is an emotional crisis related specifically, as she herself tells us, to "unrequited love." The clinical report submitted to the psychologist later described her as having made a somewhat theatrical suicide attempt in a moment of pique following an unsuccessful love affair.

Physician: But this fact was, of course, already known to the referring psychiatrist.

Psychologist: In this instance, yes, so that I used the clinical history to show *you* how it was possible to validate these completed sentences in relation to the patient's own problems. But sometimes it happens that comparable information, which has been *withheld in direct clinical interviews*, is revealed through these sentences. Sometimes a patient is very loathe to admit his most pressing problems during the initial interviews. Sometimes it is possible to cut short these resistances and delays by suggesting areas of approach to the therapist.

However, we are not only interested in specific incidents or specific information. The psychologists who developed this test stress particularly that the answers reflect ways of reacting which reach out far beyond a particular occurrence. Thus, we are talking here about a girl who is emotionally vulnerable and critically dependent on the love she receives. This is as important as is the information we are able to deduce about a crisis or incident.

Physician: Do people always finish these sentences in the same way even if they take the test after an interval of time?

Psychologist: That often depends on what has happened during the interval of time. I have two records here taken over a year apart. The first record was administered during a period of acute emotional disturbance and panic. The second, at the end of a year's therapy. I will take at random several sentences from the first record:

"A large crowd . . . *is horrible.*" "People are praised when . . . *they do nothing.*" "The hardest decisions . . . *are noise.*" "The easiest way to get money is . . . *not to do anything.*" "Few children fear . . . *fire.*" (In the Most Unpleasant Concept this patient drew the picture of fire consuming her.) "No one can repair the damage caused by . . . *me.*" "The main difference between a wild and tame animal is . . . *nothing.*" "One can hardly see . . . *anything.*" "Few things are less attractive than . . . *hope.*" "Worse than being lonely is . . . *being ashamed.*"

Now, let's see what happened to these same sentences a year later: "A large crowd . . . *gathers at the accident.*" "People are praised when . . . *they accomplish something outstanding.*" "The hardest decisions . . . *often have to be made the fastest.*" "The easiest way to get money is . . . *to work for it.*" "Few children fear . . . *adventure if they are properly prepared.*" "No one can repair the damage caused by . . . *death.*" "The main difference between a wild and tame animal is . . . *the way it reacts to a human being.*" "One can hardly see . . . *on a dark night when the lights are out.*" "Few things are less attractive than . . . *dirt.*"

Can you get a different "feel" of how the world appeared to this patient at these two different times?

Physician: Very definitely; but I don't know that I can put my finger on it. In the first record, for example, it seems to me you can feel the patient's confusion, guilt, a certain irrational quality and perhaps such a great concern with her own distress that she hardly comes to grips with the test at all on occasions. In the second presentation, all that is gone. The patient appears much more poised.

Psychologist: I would agree. Could you be more explicit and say how you arrived at those conclusions?

Physician: I thought she must feel very guilty to make a reply like, "No one can repair the damage caused by . . . *me*." And, to say that "Worse than being lonely is . . . *being ashamed*," seems to harp on the same theme. I felt she seemed confused with such an answer as, "One can hardly see . . . *anything*." It is hard to disentangle when I feel she is not really coming to grips with the test and when an answer seems irrational. It's certainly hard to follow such reasoning as, "Few things are less attractive than . . . *hope*." Nor can I make any sense out of "The hardest decisions are . . . *noise*." I think I would also say that the patient showed herself to be much more vulnerable at the time of the first testing, whereas later you get the feeling that she is quite composed and chooses answers which she considers suitable.

Psychologist: Excellent. You could also add that she seems to have shaken off the apathy that characterizes the first performance and to have reestablished goals toward which she is progressing. The blatant withdrawal from problems of living has passed over into a more realistic caution. In fact, life could even have elements of adventure if one were careful in preparing oneself for it.

Let me pick up again on your question about how information from one test ties in with another. Do you remember when I talked about the necessity of giving a series or battery of tests rather than relying on any single instrument, one of my arguments was that the test findings sometimes conflicted with each other?

Physician: When this happens does it make you feel that some tests are more reliable than others?

Psychologist: No. I think it suggests rather that the tests may penetrate to different levels of the individual but that information from any level can be instructive when weighed and assessed in terms of the total personality. I am thinking in particular in regard to the Sentence Completion Test of the possibility of highlighting conflicts. For example, consider two patients, each with a very "explosive" Rorschach record, that is, a record which showed such diffuse effect, strong instinctual drives, and too little maturity or intellectual control. For one patient, however, this can be seen to be the source of concern when in the Sentence Completion one finds, "If people only knew how much . . . *good self-restraint can do them*," or, "To be without shame . . . *ought to be impossible*." Such an individual sees himself very differently than the man who replies, "To be without shame is . . . *fun*," and "If people only knew how much . . . *good it does them to get 'tight,' they'd do it more often*."

There is another comparable situation when in the Rorschach record it can be seen that the individual finds it virtually impossible to respond emotionally or reach outward to others. You may remember the graph of the withdrawn individual where the intensity of the imaginative life was in no way offset by the hold or emotional pull of others. Sometimes the *direction* in which this emotional isolation is going can be seen from the subsidiary material of the Sentence Completion Test. One would assess two withdrawn individuals differently, for instance, if they were aware of, or disturbed about, this emotional isolation or if they did everything in their power to maintain it. For example, the withdrawn individual who answered, "Worse than being lonely is . . . *not being able to deal with loneliness*," and "If people only know how much . . . *people need people*," is facing the problem very differently from one who replies, "Worse than being lonely is . . . *there is no such thing as loneliness*." He is beginning to deny the existence of others to the extent that he will say, "There is hardly any . . . *people*." Here the sentence has become ungrammatical in order that this inner pressure may be given expression. This particular patient reinforced his need for isolation at every turn, considering himself, literally, a different species from the rest of mankind. "The kind of animal I would like to be . . . *an aardvark, the rarest known to man*."

Physician: Can you pick up contradictions within the personality from one and the same test?

Psychologist: Very readily. A frequent adolescent problem is the revolt against the parent standing side by side with the strong feelings of dependency. Look at some of the answers of this adolescent girl:

"Fathers should learn that . . . *children are not their property*." "Mothers should learn that . . . *a child has to lead a life of its own*." On the other hand, "It hurts when . . . *one is ignored*." "The kind of animal I would most like to be is . . . *a cat, because it's cuddled*."

Physician: Can you tell the patient's I.Q. from the kind of completions he makes to sentences?

Psychologist: In a very general way, you can, I think, tell the level of a patient's intellectual performance. For example, if I gave you illustrations of the record of a girl with defective intelligence, with an I.Q. somewhere around 50,

and you contrasted them with the performance of a very
superior adult, with an I.Q. around 140, you would instantly
spot which was which. For instance, take these sentences at
random:

"When an animal is wild . . . *does he scratch something?*"
"Compared with dogs . . . *cats are animals.*" "Worse than
being lonely is . . . *have nobody.*" "Children are usually certain that . . . *mommy loves me.*" Compare these with,
"When an animal is wild . . . *it enjoys the greatest freedom
but suffers the greatest risk.*" "Compared with dogs . . . *cats
are less sociable and more independent.*" "Fathers should
learn that . . . *love is more important than discipline.*"
"Worse than being lonely is . . . *being bitter.*"

Just in the verbalization and the kind of thought expressed, there is an obvious intellectual difference between
these two persons. However, these are extremes and by and
large it has always seemed to me dangerous to attempt to
make one test do the task of another. Sometimes psychologists seem to feel that unless the instrument they are particularly enthusiastic about can be shown to tell *everything*
about a person, it is not being used advantageously! It can't
be overemphasized, it seems to me, that every test has its
own area of usefulness; it can tell certain things about a patient and not others, and should be utilized with that in mind.

[VIII]

─────────────────────────────

Some Truths From Tall Tales

Psychologist: I thought you wouldn't mind, Jones, if I handled things a little differently today and combined my discussion with you with one of the sessions in an introductory course on the projective techniques which I am giving to a group of graduate students. Today you are all going to be guinea pigs together. As a matter of fact, I am conducting their class in a rather unusual and unorthodox way. They are learning about themselves at the same time as learning about the projective techniques, and they are working entirely from their own raw material or test productions.

Physician: You mean to say they can take it!

Psychologist: Well, yes. They were carefully screened before they were admitted to this particular class and, while, as I discussed earlier with you, one would never confront a seriously disturbed individual with psychopathological or clinical findings which could be derived from studying his test protocol, this group of healthy young people, several of whom have already embarked on a personal analysis in order to understand themselves better, seem to be reacting very favorably and finding it a rewarding way of working. Here they come. Let me introduce you: Dr. Jones — Mr. Rubin, Mrs. Poletsky, Mrs. Weiss, Dr. Amory, Mr. Hornbeck, and Miss Cushman. Dr. Jones, as I told you, has been interested enough in learning about the projective techniques to have had several individual sessions with me. He started out with appropriate skepticism — the kind of skepticism I encouraged each and every one of you to have, but has progressed to a point where he is going to become a clinical psychologist if we are not careful! Right, Jones?

Physician: Let's say that I am vitally interested and have got some fascinating pointers on myself into the bargain.

Psychologist: Before I start the topic of today which, incidentally, is going to be the Thematic Apperception Test or the TAT, as we familiarly call it, I think it might be interesting if each of you would tell Dr. Jones in a few words why you are taking this course, what you are particularly interested in, what your background is, and so on. Mrs. Poletsky, why don't you start?

Mrs. Poletsky: I am a marriage counselor. I work with one of the big agencies and also I have my own office and a private practice. My training was originally in social work. I don't consider myself a psychologist, although I have taken quite a few courses in the field. I hope to go on and study projective techniques intensively as I feel it might give a new dimension to some of my counseling work. I will be interested in using the material directly with my clients somewhat in the way in which we have been learning about ourselves in class. I have had some psychoanalysis, and I am finding the course very useful.

Psychologist: Mr. Hornbeck?

Mr. Hornbeck: I am a personnel manager. My training has been essentially in business. I have been with my present firm for a long time. I have a psychologist working with me in my department who employs various psychological tests. I became interested in the projective techniques by going over some of the reports. I was at first skeptical about the kind of information that was elicited and decided to understand the techniques a little better myself.

Psychologist: Dr. Amory?

Dr. Amory: I have my doctor's degree in psychology. As a matter of fact, I teach at one of the rival institutions. I am not taking the course for credit, but I really wanted to become better acquainted with the clinical point of view. I am an experimentalist myself and I think there is a danger in our profession of too great a gulf developing between those of us with a strictly experimental background and psychologists who are clinically oriented and dealing with people. As a matter of fact, I may go on to study the techniques intensively with a view to subjecting some of them to more vigorous experimental treatment than I think they have had to date.

Psychologist: Miss Cushman?

Miss Cushman: I am getting my Ph. D. in psychology and I hope to be a psychodiagnostician. I have already taken an intensive course in the Rorschach, but I spent so much time struggling with the details of the scoring system that I kind of lost track of the meaning of the test as a whole. I took the course in the hope of getting a broader perspective.

Psychologist: Mr. Rubin?

Mr. Rubin: I am also a Ph. D. candidate, but I hope to go into specialized training for psychotherapy and ultimately to open my own office. Unlike Miss Cushman, I don't expect to use the techniques myself. I probably won't go on for further training in them, but I consider a therapist should utilize all possible avenues for increased self-knowledge, and I have been particularly interested in seeing myself as the tests see me!

Psychologist: Mrs. Weiss?

Mrs. Weiss: I am just a housewife. I have grown children and I became particularly interested in psychology when one of my children majored in it. I believe now I really must have registered for the course because I thought it would help me solve some of my own personal problems. Perhaps I looked on it as sort of a substitute for some of the psychoanalysis which perhaps I should have. It seems to me I'm getting a lot out of it though.

Psychologist: Good. Now I think we can get down to the business in hand. As I said, I want to discuss the TAT or the Thematic Apperception Test with you today.

Physician: What did you say was the name of the test?

Psychologist: The Thematic Apperception Test. I don't blame you for not getting it right away. As a matter of fact, a great deal is epitomized in those words, particularly in Apperception, and to define it at this moment would not be too meaningful. Rather let's plunge into the task with which we confront the patient or the "subject," as individuals who take tests in experimental situations are frequently called. I am going to show you some pictures.*

Physician: (interrupting) Inkblot pictures? Meaningless pictures?

Psychologist: Definitely not inkblots and really not meaningless, since you will see in them people and easily recognizable objects. Perhaps one should say they are ambiguous or give you minimal information so that, in the way typical of projective techniques, you will be able to fill in as much as possible from your own reservoir of experiences, feelings, impressions, and needs.

Physician: Is my task the same as in the inkblot test, to say what I see?

Psychologist: Yes and no. To say just what you see would be too easy, too noncommital, and wouldn't allow sufficient flexibility or freedom for you to express yourself. No, what you have to do this time is to tell a story about the picture.

Physician: You mean build a story around the characters that I see?

Psychologist: Exactly. And the most important thing to remember as you construct your story is that I want to know not only what is going on in the picture, but what led up to it and what the outcome will be or, as I sometimes say, imagine yourself entering a movie in the middle of it and seeing just one scene momentarily flashed on the screen. It's now up to you to say what has happened before you came in and what is going to happen as the story develops. My students happen to be using my set of the TAT cards,

* These pictures, which closely approximate the TAT stimulus material, were drawn for me by Carol Sloane, to whom I am much indebted.

so just look at this picture, which is near enough to it so that you will get the same experience.

Physician: Here are two men engaged in an important discussion. It would seem to be taking place in a library, or perhaps a conference room, as I see there in the background something that looks like a bookcase or stacks of periodicals. The men have come there in order that they may be undisturbed and quiet because the matter at hand is a serious one. I think they are both teachers in a school or college — I was going to say medical school — but perhaps that's not important. At any rate, the fate of one of their outstanding students is at stake. He slumped very badly in his studies. They are both perplexed about it, but they feel very differently about how it should be handled. The older man is inclined to think that disciplinary action should be taken, the student reprimanded seriously, whereas the younger, who has been more exposed to psychiatric thinking, thinks the boy should be offered a chance to unburden himself and wants to see him referred to the department of student health. The younger man prevails on his colleague to try this approach, which turns out to be very successful. The student was facing a crisis in his life and was able to profit by this therapeutic assistance, resumed his normal ways of working and finally fulfilled all the hopes that his professors had for him.

That's the end of that story, but I want to try something else before you take away the picture. I want to give you another story. These are two agents in an important international spy ring. One has just passed top secret information on to the other. As a result of this, the capital city of an important nation will be blown sky high by a bomb no larger than a briefcase.

Psychologist: Tell me — why did you add the second story?

Physician: Well, as I moved along in the first, I began to recognize, if not an actual situation, things which could be said to be typical of my experience over in the hospital and medical school, and I had the feeling that you might say that it was irrevocable and inevitable that I give my experiences away in this fashion, and I just decided to tell a totally different story which has nothing to do with my experience and concerning which, under no possible stretch of the imagination could I be involved!

Psychologist: Fair enough, and we'll discuss that legitimate feeling of yours later. Take a look now at this picture and let me have your story.

Physician: The young man who's twirling his hat in such an embarrassed fashion is a physician who has come over from the local hospital to ask the old lady's permission to perform an autopsy on her husband who had just died. There has been such a long silence that he is afraid he has made a mess of things, and he is wondering what other approach he should have used to get his point across, for, being scientifically minded, he fervently believes that the autopsy is important. All of a sudden, the old lady breaks the silence, and she agrees with him that, particularly in cases of such rare diseases as that which killed her husband, an autopsy is important. She further surprises him by saying that it was her husband's wish that she give a sizeable gift of money to the hospital for specific research along these lines.

Psychologist: Obviously we don't have time for the whole series. There are, incidentally, thirty-one such pic-

tures in the entire set and, as before, we are using this procedure as an illustration. I am not trying to test you systematically. Let's have one more picture. What is your reaction to this scene? What is going on here, what has happened, and what is going to happen?

Physician: This young couple have just returned from their honeymoon and have spent the day settling into their new apartment. The man has an appointment as an intern in the local hospital and he is due to start work the next morning. They are relaxed, tired, happy, talking things over when suddenly the telephone rings. It is the hospital asking Dr. Baumann to go over there right away — there is a case in the emergency room. Dr. Baumann gets up to go immediately, but he is chiefly concerned about how his wife will take it. She surprises and reassures him murmuring in a sleepy voice, "Don't worry, old dear, I knew what I was doing when I married a doctor. Hurry up and save that life, and when you come back I'll tell you the rest of the bedtime story." I won't say they lived happily ever afterward, but they were certainly off to a good start.

Psychologist: Now, in order to provide some other and contrasting stories, I am going to suggest that we all listen to some of the material that the class accumulated as a special assignment, at this time. In addition to their giving their own responses to the TAT pictures, which they have done, each of the students had an assignment to administer the test to another subject and, in deference to Dr. Amory, we have tried to make these other subjects as homogeneous a group as possible. Let's see, what were the qualifications to be? Between twenty and twenty-one years old, male, in medical school, and with an I.Q. falling in the Very Su-

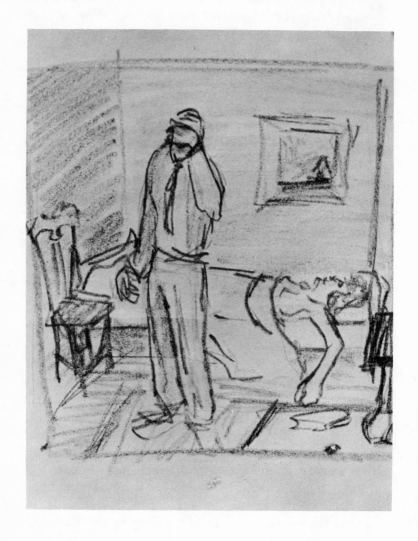

perior group of the total population, that is, between 128 and 140. What else did we stipulate, Dr. Amory?

Dr. Amory: They had to come from unbroken homes, that is, where both parents were alive and living together. They had to have at least one male and one female sibling each.

Mr. Rubin: We did this, Dr. Jones, because, since the TAT reflects primarily the subject's experiences and responses in interpersonal relationships, and since the family is the basis of such experiences, we wanted to be sure that "objectively" our six subjects belonged in comparable family constellations.

Psychologist: I think the procedure at this point is for me to read aloud some of the stories that each of you obtained. Obviously, we won't have time for all the responses, so let us select the same three pictures that Dr. Jones has told us stories about.

Story 1 — "The young man is ashamed of himself as he has shamed a woman. He appears as if he is a student of some sort because of those books. The young lady is laid out in a wanton fashion. The young man becomes very happy later when he finds out he has actually done no real harm. The young couple are married and the man finishes his studies and becomes a very distinguished individual in the line of work he chooses to do."

Story 2 — "The young couple have returned from a date and have been arguing. Finally, in his wrath, the boy strangles the girl. He then throws her body in the river and spends several years in terror and flight from the police."

Story 3 — "The girl is an attractive young woman who is very popular in school and well thought of. She suffered injuries to the lower extremities in an automobile accident and died after being carried to the hospital. The doctor has left and her father is trying to recover from his loss. He then returns home and prepares to tell his other children, who are away at college. His wife had been dead for some time, increasing the value of this daughter."

Story 4 — "The man has awakened from a drunken orgy. He is very much ashamed of himself."

Story 5 — "A young couple very much in love marry. The boy is a medical student. About the middle of the boy's freshman year, the girl — now his wife — becomes ill and dies. The boy is very upset and nearly quits school. A very understanding dean in the medical school realizes the boy's problem and by friendly advice and consultation helps him to complete the year. The boy becomes a famous doctor and later marries again and has a family."

Story 6 — "A boy of teen-age sensual thought who had unfortunately been through youth in vulgar older crowds. He grows up under sensual pleasure via thought. He is involved with a sweet girl, but he is so confused . . . his thoughts bother him so that in a fit of passion he seduces her. He realized he had lost his control and wishes he hadn't. His love is great for the girl, and hers for him. He reforms and they eventually marry."

Psychologist: Before we go any further, before I ask you for any impressions which you may have about these stories, let's see if we can give each one a name in terms of some characteristic of the hero, instead of just talking about them as students 1, 2, 3, 4, 5, and 6. What would you suggest we call the writer of story 1?

Mr. Rubin: I'd suggest "The Ashamed Young Man." He mentions that word twice in the first line.

Miss Cushman: In line with that, then, I think we should call the writer of story 2 "The Wrathful Young Man."

Physician: I think the writer of story 3, then, should be called "The Bereaved Father." There is no young man in it, and he seems to have lost his wife and child.

Dr. Amory: Story 4 seems to call itself "The Drunken Young Man."

Miss Cushman: Should we call the writer of story 5 "The Famous Young Man"?

Mrs. Poletsky: I think that the writer of the last story should be called "The Confused Young Man." I'd have some more to say about him later.

Psychologist: Any reactions or first impressions for these stories before we go on to their other examples?

Physician: I find it hard to believe that we, the students and I, are starting from the same scene. For instance, the one we call "The Drunken Young Man" writes a story, if you can call it a story, about only one person in the picture. He completely disregards the fact that there is a girl in the scene too. "The Bereaved Father" writing about his daughter would seem to be in a completely different age-group from the young couples mentioned by some of the other writers. And it seems to me as if I would have to envisage several completely different girls, one dead, one injured, one recently seduced, and so on.

Mrs. Poletsky: I am struck by the difference in style. Or perhaps I mean more than style. The last story you read seemed so extraordinarily confused. It seemed as if this young man didn't make sense or give complete sentences. In contrast to this, the one we described as "The Ashamed

Young Man" seemed to be much more logical. He deduces, for instance, that the man must be a student because he sees books in the background. Then there is a story which is just a bare skeleton — a single sentence, no elaboration of thought at all.

Psychologist: That's a very good observation, and let's proceed to the other stories with this in mind. We might ask whether "The Drunken Young Man" stayed true to form while reacting or supposedly building his story around the other two pictures.

Mr. Hornbeck: I have his record here. I wouldn't have believed it. His story for the picture with the two men is this: "The man in this scene has gotten into trouble. He is found guilty and sentenced." His story for the picture with the older woman and the man is simply: "In this scene, a man is breaking some news to a woman."

Psychologist: We would have to agree, I think, that if we are paying attention only to the style in which the story is written, there is an unmistakable similarity among all these productions. The very minimum response to the requirements of the test is given. As we shall see later, this is only one of many ways in which a story can be assessed or evaluated, but we do seem to have found a common denominator here. Dr. Amory, whose record do you have, and would you read the stories in the same order?

Dr. Amory: I have here the stories of "The Confused Young Man." "In the beginning the boy came from a poor family and had dissipated as a playboy. A man's attitude toward life changes after my friend had been killed. The boy then talks to his very rich uncle who has brought him up. He decides to reform and renounces it all."

And the other story reads as follows: "The boy has been going with a rich girl (and the word "rich" is crossed out) who is interested only in his money. The boy did not think straight and was upset. He lost all his money in the stock market crash and has just told his girl. The girl has walked out on him. After the boy started a new life, realizes she loves him, leaves home, and marries him. The maid has come in to show him out." I certainly think he lives up to his name of Mr. Confusion!

Psychologist: Yes, and I think we have to distinguish between a certain confusion in sentence structure and a confusion or an ambivalence in his thinking. Did anybody notice anything special about these stories?

Miss Cushman: I think it was very interesting and very strange how he suddenly inserted the first person in the middle of the sentence. He talked about *my* friend being killed.

Mrs. Poletsky: There seems to be some real confusion about money or as if he can't decide, even for the boy in the story, whether he comes from a wealthy or poor family.

Mr. Rubin: I think it's interesting how in the second story — the one with the man and the elderly woman — he almost didn't react to the picture at all! At the very last minute he saves himself by bringing in the maid. Up to that point, however, nothing that he said in the story really related to the picture.

Dr. Amory: Just one more point. This confused young man seems to use words so strangely. He states, for example, he had been "dissipated as a playboy." There seems to be a confusion of two ideas or he puts two ways of saying something into one.

Psychologist: Who shall we take next?

Miss Cushman: I have the stories here of the student we called "The Wrathful Young Man." To call him wrathful from his first story is probably an understatement, since he was the one who strangled his girl and threw her body in the river. These are the stories he gives to the other two pictures. "The older man is taking a fatherly interest in the younger. Probably he has just given him some advice. The old man appears sure the advice is good and that it will be accepted. However, the younger man is thinking just the opposite. He gets furious at the way he is being nagged at and he jumps up and slams the door; he leaves that night to go out West and start his own business." His other story is: "The young man has had a successful time in educational circles and has been called up for induction into the army. However, he doesn't go to the induction center. He sees a liner tied up in port, jumps ship and sails for the Orient as a stowaway. No one discovers him until it is far too late to put him off the boat. In the Orient he makes a great success."

Mrs. Poletsky: Well, I really don't feel that I could say that these three stories are similar in style to each other in the way that the stories of "The Drunken Young Man" or "The Confused Young Man" have been.

Mr. Rubin: I wonder if the similarity here isn't in the fact that the hero acts so impulsively. It is true that he commits a murder only in the first story, but look how he gets furious and slams the door and leaves for the West in the second, and jumps on a ship and sails for the Orient in the third.

Dr. Amory: There seems to be a common denominator here in that the hero somehow assumes that if he can get away from the present situation everything is going to be fine. I don't feel the hero in these stories is too realistic. He looks for too easy solutions.

Psychologist: As far as style is concerned, then, we don't feel that he has left his imprint in the way he writes as much as the fact that his irritability, wrath, and impulsiveness seem to show up in all the stories. I think we have time for one more.

Mrs. Weiss: I have here the stories of the one we called "The Famous Young Man," and I would like to read them. I like his attitude very much. "A young boy wishes to attend a medical school, but his father wants him to go into the family business. However, the boy leaves home and attempts to work his way through school. He finds much of his ambition gone since he no longer has his father's friendship, so he returns home and he and his father get together and his father is really keen on his doing well in a medical career. So he goes back to school with his father's blessing and does extremely well. The dean writes to his father that the boy's progress is quite unusual and that he has a great career ahead of him." And his other story: "A coal miner's son has been working in the coal mines since he was fourteen. All his life he has wanted to go to college, so he works in the summer and finally has enough money to go. He packs his things and then goes into the kitchen to tell his mother. She wants him to go because she believes in him. He does well in college, becomes a respected citizen, and then turns to a political career. He runs for various offices and finally is nominated for the President of the United States."

Psychologist: Tell me a little bit about the hero of these stories, Mrs. Weiss, and why you like him.

Mrs. Weiss: What I find the same in these stories — well, let me put it this way — so many young people these days seem to think the older generation's got it in for them. They want to get away from home. Now this boy, or the people he writes about, seem to need to get on well with the father and the mother.

Dr. Amory: You could say, also, that he extends this attitude toward other authority figures. For instance, he speaks of "a very understanding dean in medical school" in the first story. Whatever this boy's problems are, they don't seem to relate to getting on with his elders.

Psychologist: How about the style in these stories?

Mrs. Poletsky: I'd have to admit that these stories are not sufficiently different in their way of writing so that I could tell them from the stories of "The Impulsive Young Man." I would, of course, find them quite different from those of "The Drunken Young Man" and "The Confused Young Man."

Psychologist: I think that you have all had a sufficient opportunity to react spontaneously to the stimulus material of the TAT, and, equally important, you've had the chance to see how others produce stories or *themes* or can "Apperceive Thematically" in a way quite different from your own.

The name, the Thematic Apperception Test, will now make more sense to you, for this is a test whereby you perceive and interpret, or apperceive, pictures in such a way as to develop themes or stories out of the "mere" picture. It is true that the picture is not meaningless, in the sense that the inkblots are, so that you are not giving all the meaning to the picture by your stories. But, as you have seen, the pictures are ambiguous, in varying degrees, allowing many legitimate interpretations. The one you construct is the meaning it has for *you*.

Physician: Who was the Dr. Rorschach of the TAT, if I may put it that way?

Psychologist: You may! The originator of the TAT was Dr. Henry Murray, who in 1936, together with Christiana Morgan, wrote an article on what they called "A Method of Investigating Fantasies" which set the ball rolling.

Miss Cushman: If the test is used in a diagnostic battery what would you say it reveals better than other tests?

Psychologist: Perhaps the most important thing that the TAT can give us — and I think you will agree in the light of some of the themes we have looked at today — is insight into how an individual sizes up and reacts to a variety of social situations. This, of course, means that the test is directed to a study of interpersonal relations. Almost inevitably from the stories that are given we get information on how the individual envisages or reacts to the older, parental figures in his environment, his peers, or, if he is an older person, we get insights into his orientation toward, and expectancies from, the younger generation.

You would agree, I think, that it is possible to ask about a young writer such questions as, "Does he envisage his elders as people who threaten him? Support him? Reinforce him and help him?" And so on.

Physician: Is the test "scored" like the Rorschach?

Psychologist: No, not exactly, but various attempts have been made to analyze the material and to extract the common denominators from the stories. It would seem as if the original scoring method devised by Murray and Morgan met with somewhat less universal acceptance than did Rorschach's suggestions for his inkblots. The scoring of a projective technique, I may say, always constitutes a problem, as anyone who has attempted to devise a test well knows. For if you are too systematic, too punctilious, too careful in an attempt to give a quantitative score to every little item, you may make the procedure so complicated that even though people may be willing to learn it, they do not have time to use it. If, however, you are not able to introduce some order, some means of classifying, grouping, and arranging the test results from your various testees, or persons examined by your methods, then, while you, yourself, may be able to use it at an intuitive level, you cannot convey or pass on to students or interested colleagues a systematic body of knowledge.

The TAT has been subjected to several alternative interpretive schemes. Murray and Morgan, for instance attempted to analyze every sentence in every story in terms of the things which the hero needed, and the extent to which the environment (of course, including all the other people in the environment) resisted his needs, pressured or, to use Murray's words, pressed him.

Physician: What sort of needs, what sort of forces from the environment?

Psychologist: Picking at random from Murray's list, one might have, for example, the need for respect, the need to achieve, the need for change, the need for recognition, the need for seclusion, the need for sex, and the environment can press back with forces such as punishment, physical injury, failure, accomplishment, and a host of others.

At the other extreme from this rather detailed, or piece-meal treatment of the story, it is possible to find meaning in the stories without any attempt at systematic classification or scoring. Almost invariably, if one reads through ten or fifteen stories by the same individual, one finds (as we have just seen in some of the students' stories) a repetitive pattern running through them. The more one knows about projective material, for instance, the more one is able to pick up the suggestive clues, always remembering, however — and this is something that has been stressed so often in our discussions — that no single answer merits a clinical judgment or decision in or of itself. It is only when a repetitive pattern begins to emerge that we are sure we are not dealing with what may be an artifact or something very insignificant in the total makeup of the individual.

Physician: Is it necessary for me to learn a scoring system here in order to understand psychological reports that use this test?

Psychologist: No, but I think it would be worthwhile to subject your own story to the scheme of interpretation that has been suggested by Bellak, which is a sort of middle of the road type of interpretation; a process that allows a common denominator to be detected in the various stories without going into exhaustive detail.

Among the things Bellak suggests we look for are these: We should determine the age, sex, and vocation of the main hero or heroine of the story, and acquaint ourselves with his interests, traits, abilities, and the adequacy that he shows in achieving his objective. Then we should look at his attitudes to superiors and to society. Is it autonomous, grateful, resistant, compliant, dependent, aggressive, respectful, remorseful, devoted, competitive, or fearful? Having determined this, we should study the figures which are introduced into the story, even though the picture does not show them. Are such figures punishers, friends, enemies, pursuers, performers, benefactors, lovers, teachers, supporters, and so on? We should concern ourselves with objects which are introduced and consider their possible symbolic value. We should be concerned with objects which have been omitted. As we continue to look at the story, we should see whether blame is attached to anyone. Is there injustice, do we find unfortunate influences, deception, indifference, deprivation? Do we find the hero expressing any significant conflicts? Do the stories involve punishment? Is it just, too severe, lenient; does it come immediately; is it delayed, or is there none? We should look at the attitude that the storyteller takes toward his hero. Is it, for instance, detached and objective, critical and abusive, or involved and empathic? Is the outcome of the story happy, unhappy, realistic, or unrealistic? Is the plot structured or unstructured, realistic or bizarre, complete or incomplete?

Mrs. Poletsky: Can we make this scheme more concrete by trying it out on one of the stories?

Psychologist: Of course, let's see what we can do in assessing one of Dr. Jones's stories according to Bellak's Analysis Sheet. Who was the main hero in this instance?

Mrs. Poletsky: I think you'd have to say that there were two main heroes — two colleagues, middle-aged and younger, their vocation obviously medicine. Their interests seem to be scholarly, educational, or perhaps pedagogical, and psychiatric. One may be said to be more open-minded than the other. I would say they seem completely adequate to the task in hand.

Psychologist: Any comments, Dr. Jones?

Physician: No, I think I'd go along with that.

Mrs. Poletsky: About their attitudes to their juniors or inferiors, I think they are concerned and responsible. Concerning the figure introduced, it would, of course, be the student.

Dr. Amory: About those objects introduced — stacks of periodicals — frankly, I can't see them.

Physician: (laughing) No, they're not there. That's one I'll have to discuss with you later.

Dr. Amory: There are, however, no objects omitted as far as I can see. How about blame?

Physician: Yes, I think the older of the two blames the student, perhaps not too severely.

Psychologist: What would you say were the significant conflicts?

Dr. Amory: I think there is a suggestion of conflict in that the teller of the story gives himself the opportunity, through the two characters, to be both authoritarian and therapeutic.

Mrs. Poletsky: I think from the analytic point of view one might say that the colleague who is recommending discipline represents the more masculine side of the storyteller, while the psychiatrically minded one suggests the more tender, feminine, or compliant side of him.

Psychologist: How would we answer the query about punishment in the story?

Mr. Hornbeck: There would be no punishment.

Psychologist: The attitude to the hero, or heroes?

Dr. Amory: I think I would vote for involved and empathic.

Miss Cushman: No, I think it is detached and objective.

Psychologist: Perhaps we can settle for it being objective with some empathy also shown. And what about the outcome of the story?

Mrs. Weiss: I think it's a happy ending. It also seems to me to be quite realistic.

Psychologist: Would you say the story was structured or unstructured, realistic or bizarre, complete or incomplete?

Dr. Amory: I think we'd have to answer that it is structured, realistic, and complete.

Psychologist: Let's compare this story with one that will give the greatest contrast. Let's take the story of the young man we described as wrathful and impulsive. The main hero is obviously a young man. His present vocation is unspecified. His interests seem to be in business. Regarding his traits, he gets angry, acts out his anger, and acts impulsively. We really do not know his abilities or his adequacies. His attitude toward his superior is resentful; no figures are introduced; no objects are introduced; no objects are omitted; blame is certainly attributed to the father for "nagging." There may be some conflict here between superego and id or, in less formidable terms, between his feeling that he ought to listen to his father and his need to satisfy his own wishes. There is no punishment for the crime; one is led to assume that the business out West prospers. There is no

question, I think, but that the attitude of the hero is involved and empathic, the outcome happy, but somewhat
unrealistic.

Psychologist: This may be a good moment for me to present a somewhat different point of view from the one I
have espoused up to now in my discussions with Dr. Jones
and in my preliminary lectures in class. Since these talks
were an introduction to the projective techniques, I main-
tained an attitude indicating belief in their usefulness and
happily ignoring the critics and the critical lines of attack to
which each of these tests can be, and have been, subjected.

As beginners, either from psychology or medicine, it is
necessary that you get an overall picture of what the individual who devised the test strove for or aimed to do with
it, even if he did not always succeed, and even if later
generations could point to erroneous assumptions that were
contained therein. It is also necessary for those of you who
will use the tests clinically to be capable of drawing information from them which is relevant for you in your therapeutic capacity. For there is no getting away from the fact
that even if we do not always understand how or why a test
works, we must be open-minded enough to accept help
from it in clinical situations.

Physician: The same thing is true in medicine, of course.
We sometimes find ourselves using medication that alleviates
the patient's suffering, even though the exact chemical action is not understood. Diagnostically, of course, the EEG
was helpful in locating brain lesions long before its theoretical implications were understood.

Mr. Rubin: Since I expect to use the tests therapeutically,
as you say, or in my therapeutic practice, can you give a

specific example of what you mean by help?

Psychologist: Yes, I consider that one case of mine was materially and dramatically facilitated by its use of one particular point. I was treating a girl who was anxious and depressed. She was not making much progress. On a number of occasions I had administered the TAT to her, or some cards from it. Her reaction to one of them in particular interested me for, although most individuals see two women in it, my patient persistently spoke of a girl and a boy and told some short noncommital story in connection with it. Then one day she told a story about two girls — two sisters, as a matter of fact — and how they hated each other, and how one of them always undermined and ruined the other's chances in life, particularly, with their male friends. When the patient put down this card she turned very white and exclaimed, as if making the most important discovery of her life, "Why, I'm talking about my sister!" From then on our therapeutic work speeded up miraculously until this patient was finally able to face up to these buried feelings of distrust and jealousy of her sister, which she had kept hidden from herself until that time.

Mrs. Poletsky: Why do you think she was able to change her story at that point and come to grips with her problem?

Psychologist: I am not sure why on that particular day, but I would assume that over the months she had been building up a certain trust in the relationship between herself and her therapist so that, finally, this dangerous material could be brought to light. But this question leads us to the kind of things that can be handled experimentally and concerning which there are now hypotheses which relate in turn to understanding the test, itself.

Dr. Amory: Are you referring to some of the experimental work discussed at a recent conference dealing with problems in the TAT?

Psychologist: Yes. Why don't you tell us about it, particularly as it relates to this case.

Dr. Amory: Well, as I understand it, the suggestion is that when a story or a theme that could be told is too "hot," too close to the live issues for that person, it arouses at the same time so much anxiety that the anxiety inhibits the development of that theme and another story is told in its place — a story which very frequently distorts some aspect of the picture itself.

Miss Cushman: This would mean to me that the test would not be at all what I thought it was going to be. I would have suspected that the things the individual didn't dare to bring up himself, but which were pressuring him very greatly, would be just those things that he would tell his story about.

Psychologist: This is exactly the kind of issue to which the experimentalists have to give us an answer. Those of us who have used the projective techniques rather too blithely assumed that they all reached down into the individual's unconscious and brought up material which gave the "real" picture of him, so that we were then in possession of the truth. There should be a constant modification going on of the tests we use, the conclusions we draw from them, as our understanding of them deepens and sharpens by virtue of systematic experimental studies which can be made.

Dr. Amory: In this instance, then, you could say that the perception of the picture, the apperception of the picture, actually changed with the reduction in anxiety, and a theme that had always been potentially very pertinent and revealing was able to come to consciousness. From then on, it was grist for the therapist's mill.

Mr. Hornbeck: I'd like to ask a question, and perhaps you can tie it into your present discussion, so that I don't upset your line of thought. I don't remember the picture that you speak about, but wouldn't it make some difference if your patient had given her story to a picture that was hazy and ambiguous, and in which the sex of the two individuals was not sharply delineated? If she kept on giving the story about a man and a woman where the picture was "obviously" of two women, doesn't that tell you something different?

Psychologist: The answer is "Yes." The experimental work I spoke of that is being done in the field of clinical psychology is concentrating on this very difference between what is elicited from a truly ambiguous picture, and from one that has much more structure. I have a quotation here which bears directly on what you say. "An early error made by many clinicians involved the assumption that the TAT picture was sufficiently vague and ambiguous that its manifest perceptual meanings could be ignored in the evaluation of the story content. This is one of the more serious errors that has been made in the history of psychological methods. Study after study has demonstrated that the objective nature of the picture dictates much of the content, and prediction can be improved if the ambiguity of the stimulus for specific contents is carefully assessed. Moreover, some contents — aggression, for example — have different predictive significance if they occur in an ambiguous stimulus, if they occur to an ambiguous stimulus, and if they are associated with a stimulus which does not suggest the content in question."* To go back to my original example, when my patient looked at the picture which was not ambiguous, but which showed quite clearly that two girls were involved, then you would say the pressure to make one of them a male figure or, conversely, not to make both of them female, could be considered greater than if such a story had only occurred as a reaction to a more ambiguous picture.

Mrs. Weiss: Could you tell me again what you mean by an ambiguous picture?

Psychologist: The dictionary tells us that ambiguity is a quality of being ambiguous, obscure, uncertain in meaning, especially where either of two interpretations is possible. One of the neatest experimental ambiguous figures is this one. What does it look like to you, Mrs. Weiss?

Mrs. Weiss: It looks like the profiles of two people.

Psychologist: And to you, Mrs. Poletsky?

Mrs. Poletsky: To me, it looks like a vase.

Psychologist: Exactly. Now I can do things to this to make it less ambiguous. By putting dots here, I would reinforce the experience of the profiles, and by putting lines here, I would reinforce the experience of the vase.** Now I think you would agree that it means something different,

* Kagan, Jerome, and Lesser, Gerald S.: *Contemporary Issues in Thematic Apperceptive Methods*, Charles C. Thomas, Springfield, Illinois, 1961.
** Harrower, Molly: "Changes in Figure-Ground Perception in Patients with Cortical Lesions." *British Journal of Psychology*. Vol. XXX, Part 1, 1939.

or it is a different experience if you continue to see the profiles, even when I augment the vase and vice versa. An ambiguous picture on the TAT would be one where the scene that is presented is capable of multiple interpretations.

Mr. Rubin: One of the stories of our medical students bothered me — the one that dealt with a murder. I think if I had not been forewarned, I might have been obliged to interpret the test as that of someone who had actually committed the murder.

Psychologist: But luckily your common sense comes to your rescue, and you know that isn't true. Does it then have any truth? We saw that it belonged to a group of stories by an individual who seemed to repeat a theme of irritability, angriness, frustration, and impulsive action. If you look through the rest of the twenty cards that you gave him and find the same sort of theme, you would, I think, be prepared to admit that this might be one of his character traits and, consequently, one of his problems. But the murder story might well fit into something that we spoke of before, namely, had it by some fantastic chance been true, it is unlikely that it would have appeared in the story. Some psychologists would add to this the fact that it appears in the story, because it is safe to write it in a story and it gets rid of, or discharges, some of the wrathful and "murderous" impulses which this individual has. Or, as one psychologist puts it, "If a need has been adequately expressed in actual life striving, it would not be expressed in apperceptive fantasy, except under special conditions which are not yet clear."

Physician: Doesn't this, in some way, link up with our discussion of the Szondi Test wherein you showed us that we picked or were psychologically hungry for those faces that were caricatures of the stresses and strains which were not finding satisfaction or discharge in actual behavior?

Psychologist: Yes, I think I said just that. When some of the faces were never picked it could mean one of two things. Either that you happen to be someone without the corresponding drive in your makeup, or that in the life situation in which you find yourself, the environment was such that that particular need was constantly satiated. One might build a bridge, then, between these two tests on the assumption that one would be least likely to give stories about inner experiences that were constantly satiated by the environment.

Dr. Jones, I wonder if you would be willing to do something for us that I think only you can do, since none of the other storytellers are here with us. Could you go over your story in your mind and let us in on some of the thoughts and experiences you had in telling it? You may well find that you don't wish to reveal everything that you thought of in the sifting process, but we'll naturally respect your privacy. Just let us in on the fact if something personal and relevant took place.

Physician: As I remember, when I first looked at the picture I said to myself, "There are two men, one is slightly older than I am, one is slightly younger."

Psychologist: In other words, you weren't quite sure who you really lined yourself up with or identified with, as we say.

Physician: No. As a matter of fact, what I think crossed my mind very quickly was, I am probably nearer the age of the older one, but he's too old, he's really not me. Having started with two men and looking at the picture again, it seemed to me that they must be talking. So it's as if I said, "Talking about what?" I think what happened then was that I said to myself, "Colleagues talk about three things — their work, their family lives, and their students." At this point I remembered I had talked only yesterday with one of my colleagues about a student who was doing badly. Suddenly the story was there.

Psychologist: But you elaborated it a lot more.

Physician: Well, I can tell you one thing — the reason why I chose to say these people were speaking in a place that was undisturbed and quiet was because recently I have been bothered by constant interruptions while I have been trying to prepare an article for one of the medical journals. That's an out and out need for you; I need solitude at the present time! I then said something about the fact that it must be a library because of the stack of periodicals. I see quite clearly that they're not there, and you all picked this up when you made that survey of my story before. Frankly, I don't know why I put that in. It must be in some way related to this feeling of pressure I have about not getting my articles into periodicals quickly enough. In deciding the fate of the student, I think I can tell you that I let the younger, more flexible and less rigid part of myself win out in the discussion as to who should handle the student.

Mrs. Poletsky: How about the happy ending, Dr. Jones?

Physician: Well, I think I'd have to admit that I am pretty much of an optimist, which I am sure is no term for a psychologist to use. Perhaps I'd prefer not to look at the more unpleasant things in life, the failures of people and techniques and scientific endeavors.

Mr. Rubin: Your other stories ended happily too, Dr. Jones.

Physician: Yes, they did, and I would accept that as something which you would be permitted to use in describing my character. But I'll have to tell you that, whereas the happy ending in the story of the doctor seeking the autopsy is complete wishful thinking, I just do wish some old lady would leave us money for research — the happy ending in the bedroom scene is more or less taken from my direct experience. Those are not the exact words my wife used twenty years ago, but she said something encouraging and helpful when I was called on my first night emergency.

Mrs. Poletsky: Dr. Jones, how about the second story that you told to the first picture — the one about international spies?

Physician: Ah, yes. I did that deliberately because it seemed to me quite impossible that every story should be equally revealing. I wanted to test you or, rather, I was becoming disturbed because it seemed to me impossible that every single thing revealed by the patient, by your subjects, or by my own exposures could be equally relevant. I am sure you can find something in the international spy story that has to do with me, but I guess what I was trying to demonstrate was that not all scenes are equally meaningful.

And I am reassured by the discussion that we have been having that an oversimplification hasn't crept in, so that you, a psychologist, feel compelled to read deep meaning equally into everything.

Mr. Hornbeck: I would agree with you, Dr. Jones. I am reminded of that line in Gilbert and Sullivan, "When everybody's somebody, then no one's anybody."

Miss Cushman: I think there's another popular quotation that makes sense here, and that is, "If the cap fits, wear it." In writing reports in which I may use the TAT, I think I would be most tempted to give the stories themselves to the therapists who had referred the patients to me, perhaps pointing out the consistencies in themes or style, stressing what had been omitted and added, as far as the pictures were concerned. But I think, now, I would find myself rather wary of stating just which themes reflected the crucial needs or pressures in the individual I had examined. Perhaps I can get around this by using those TAT themes which reinforce material from some of the other tests administered at the same time.

Psychologist: A very wise principle and conclusion, Miss Cushman. And as for you Dr. Jones, I feel that you have come to the point where you've been "exposed" to a sufficient number of tests so as to have a background for a more detailed understanding of a psychological report. The next stage, I think, if you are still interested, is for you to see what some of your own patients "look like" through these instruments. With your own personal performance as a base line and a few good cases that you know well from the clinical point of view, you should soon have a frame of reference that will allow you to understand our evaluations and psychodiagnostic appraisals!

Physician: You'll be hearing from me. I have a number of cases in mind right now.

PART THREE

[1]

Which Twin Has Epilepsy?

MEDICAL BUILDING
Main St.
Hightown

Dear Smith:

After having been exposed to your test material, I find myself eager to send you a couple of patients to see how they look "from the inside."

To start my series, I have, I think, a rather fascinating case. I have just seen in the office two eleven-year-old boys, twins. One has epilepsy; the other is quite normal. Looking at them, I can't tell the difference between them and I am sure you will not be able to either. How about putting them both through your battery of tests to see whether they look different psychologically?

Although I am enclosing the case history, I am not going to tell you which of the twins is the patient. I shall eagerly await your report and please don't forget to document it with any of the raw material which you can conveniently include.

Cordially yours,
Robert Jones, M. D.

[223]

CASE HISTORY OF TWIN WITH EPILEPSY

Chief Complaint: Convulsive seizures for nine years.

Family History: There is no reported convulsive disorder in the parents, three siblings, or the identical twin. Inquiry into prior antecedents is equally unrewarded.

Development: The product of a fifth pregnancy, normal in duration, normal in termination without the use of instruments, the patient was the second of a pair of identical twins. Color, respiration and feeding immediately after delivery were normal. Both twins sat up about the fifth month, walked about the twelfth, and talked about the twenty-fourth month. There was little to distinguish one from the other except a tendency to left-handedness in the patient. Some effort was made to correct this. Both started school at five and a half and are presently in the fifth grade. Both do well, with the patient showing not quite as good grades for the past two years as his twin brother.

Childhood Illnesses: Included measles, scarlet fever, whooping cough, mumps, and chicken pox. Immunization was effected against smallpox and diphtheria.

Operations and Accidents: None — other than that mentioned in present illness.

Present Illness: At one and a half years of age (1940) the patient fell off the back step striking his head against a stone. No loss in consciousness, laceration, or contusion are reported. About one and a half hours after the incident, there was a convulsive seizure, the principal parts remembered being a straightening out with rolling back of the eyes. He was put in hot water, this being thought an acceptable remedy. During the following week there were seven convulsions. It was thought that many of these were triggered off by bumping the head.

Examination: An alert and cooperative lad without undue concern over the recurrent seizures. Gait is without abnormality. Romberg negative. There is no evidence of cerebellar or vestibular dysfunction. Calvarium and spine show no surface abnormality. Cranial nerves show no defect (tonsils are enlarged). Motor system shows no loss or inequality in muscular power, volume, or tone. Sensory system is intact to touch, pain, vibration, and position sense. There is no astereognosis.

Electroencephalogram: Without abnormality in routine record. With hyperventilation there is prompt 3/sec. slow wave activity in the patient and delayed 3/sec. activity in his brother. Mother and three siblings show moderate abnormality with hyperventilation.

Social History: (The following report was obtained through the social service from the patient's aunt.) One and one-half years ago, the father "brushed the child with his car as he backed out of the garage but did not knock him down." The father then scolded the child severely and the child immediately had a generalized convulsive seizure. He has had several seizures since that time with three seizures last week, one occurring at night, and one occurring at mealtime. The seizures seemed to be characterized by a feeling of numbness, followed by generalized weakness. My informant believes that these seizures frequently follow emotional upsets such as examinations or untoward duties.

Emotional Response: Dissimilar. The patient considered to be introspective for the past two or three years.

PROFESSIONAL BUILDING
Front St.
Hightown

Dear Jones:

Thank you for referring this fascinating case. My report on these boys follows. There can be very little doubt from the psychological tests that *Johnny is the patient with epilepsy*, although I shall naturally be eager for your confirmation. More than the diagnosis, however, I am interested in the chance to demonstrate to you how *very different are the psychological worlds* of these two boys. In regard to the case history, I should like to make one comment in the light of our original discussion. You will notice that all that is recorded for "Emotional Response" in the medical report is the statement that the twins are dissimilar, the patient having been considered "introspective for the last two or three years." This is a nice example of how psychological tests can amplify the total clinical picture. The word "introspective" which, I take it, is not used in its technical sense, can be expanded considerably through systematic psychological examination.

Thanks again for the chance to see these boys.

Sincerely yours,
John Smith, Ph.D.

PSYCHODIAGNOSTIC APPRAISAL OF
JOHNNY AND TOMMY BLANK

Introductory Remarks: Neither of these boys was referred as "the patient" and the examiner has no idea which has the clinical symptoms. No questions were asked of their mother. Both boys were given exactly the same testing battery. Tommy was examined first, and during this time Johnny took a subsidiary Sentence Completion Test administered by another psychologist in an adjoining room. When Tommy had been tested, Johnny was called in.

Observation of Behavior during Testing Period: Both boys were extremely alert and interested in the examiner's possessions and apartment. Both asked questions in regard to the paintings on the walls and the record albums. Both made a point of looking out of the window, and both were equally poised and friendly. In the examining room, however, there was a difference in the way the boys addressed themselves to the task. Tommy was eagerness itself; Johnny a little quieter and less excited. Since Johnny had been taking the subsidiary test prior to entry, this might be due to the fact that he was slightly fatigued, more likely to the fact that the newness of the situation had by that time worn off.

Evaluation of Material with Reference to Intelligence: Both boys have Good-Average scores on the verbal Wechsler-Bellevue. Both fall into the High Average Group of the total population. There is a minor difference of a few points between the two, Johnny having a Verbal I.Q. of 119, Tommy of 113. The essential fact, however, is the similarity of both scores rather than this minor difference.

However, these scores are obtained through totally different subtest patterns. The similarity between the boys and

TABLE OF WEIGHTED SCORES†

Equivalent Weighted Score	Information	Comprehension	Digit Span	Arithmetic	Similarities	Vocabulary	Picture Arrangement	Picture Completion	Block Design	Object Assembly	Digit Symbol	Equivalent Weighted Score
						RAW SCORE						
18	25	20		14	23-24	41-42	20+		38+			18
17	24	19	17	13	21-22	39-40	20		38	26		17
16	23	18	16	12	20	37-38	19		35-37	25	66-67	16
15	21-22	17		11	19	35-36	18	15	33-34	24	62-65	15
14	20	16	15		17-18	32-34	16-17	14	30-32	23	57-61	14
13	18-19	15	14	10	16	29-31	15	13	28-29	22	53-36	13
12	(17)	14		9	15	27-28	14	12	25-27	20-21	49-52	12
11	15-16	12-13	(13)		13-14	25-26	12-13		23-24	19	45-48	11
10	13-14	11	12	8	12	22-24	11	11	20-22	(18)	41-44	10
9	12	10	11	7	11	20-21	(10)	(10)	18-19	17	37-40	9
8	10-11	9			(9-10)	17-19	9	9	16-17	16	33-36	8
7	9	8	10	6	8	15-16	7-8	8	13-15	14-15	29-32	7
6	7-8	7	9	5	7	12-14	6	7	(11-12)	13	24-28	6
5	6	(5-6)			5-6	10-11	5		8-10	12	(20-23)	5
4	4-5	4	8	(4)	4	7-9	4	6	6-7	10-11	16-19	4
3	2-3	3	7	3	3	5-6	2-3	5	3-5	9	12-15	3
2	1	2	6		1-2	3-4	1	4	1-2	8	8-11	2
1	0	1		2	0	1-2	0	3	0	7	4-7	1
0		0	5	1		0		2		5-6	0-3	0

Chart IX A. Wechsler-Bellevue Scattergram of Tommy

their ways of operating ends abruptly here. The performance I.Q. for Tommy is 107, for Johnny, 108. The total I.Q. for Tommy is 110, for Johnny, 114. Tommy is much more erratic, for as his scores in the accompanying diagram illustrate, he achieves a maximum that is higher than Johnny's, but also falls considerably below Johnny in two areas. Tommy has much "scatter," namely a swing of performance through points 12 to 4 on the weighted scale of 18; Johnny's performance, on the other hand, is much more uniform, his score varying only between 11 and 8 on the weighted scale. Intellectually, then, Johnny is much more all of one piece, whereas Tommy deviates to extremes.

A breakdown of the subtests reveals that both boys have identical Memory capacities. Both can repeat the surprising number of 9 digits forward and both fail after 4 backward. In the other subtests their performance is markedly different. Tommy, for example, has an astonishing fund of knowledge for so young a boy. His information is accurate, and his responses fast and sure. Johnny is definitely less well-informed. For example, he does not know how many pints there are in a quart. Johnny is more conscientious in the sense that he makes attempts to answer even when he does not know, but his actual available fund of knowledge is definitely less than Tommy's. On the other hand, Johnny is better at Arithmetic, not only avoiding one or two of Tommy's careless slips but making an attempt on the more difficult problems which Tommy sloughs off as impossible. Johnny is also distinctly better in Abstract Thinking, coming up with more mature and adult solutions.

Johnny is also better, slightly, in the Comprehension, Reasoning, and Judgment, addressing himself more realistically to the problem.

From the point of view of the theoretical interest in examining twins, it is worthwhile to record that several answers were identical. For example, the similarity between an egg and a seed is for both children that "chickens eat seeds in order to have eggs."

Performance scale: There is much greater similarity between the performances of Tommy and Johnny on the five

TABLE OF WEIGHTED SCORES†

Equivalent Weighted Score	Information	Comprehension	Digit Span	Arithmetic	Similarities	Vocabulary	Picture Arrangement	Picture Completion	Block Design	Object Assembly	Digit Symbol	Equivalent Weighted Score
18	25	20		14	23-24	41-42	20+		38+			18
17	24	19	17	13	21-22	39-40	20			26		17
16	23	18	16	12	20	37-38	19		35-37	25	66-67	16
15	21-22	17		11	19	35-36	18	15	33-34	24	62-65	15
14	20	16	15		17-18	32-34	16-17	14	30-32	23	57-61	14
13	18-19	15	14	10	16	29-31	15	13	28-29	22	53-56	13
12	17	14		9	15	27-28	14	12	25-27	20-21	49-52	12
11	15-16	12-13	13		13-14	25-26	12-13		23-24	19	45-48	11
10	13-14	11	12	8	12	22-24	11	11	20-22	18	41-44	10
9	12	10	11	7	11	20-21	10	10	18-19	17	37-40	9
8	10-11	9			9-10	17-19	9	9	16-17	16	33-36	8
7	9	8	10	6	8	15-16	7-8	8	13-15	14-15	29-32	7
6	7-8	7	9	5	7	12-14	6	7	11-12	13	24-28	6
5	6	5-6			5-6	10-11	5		8-10	12	20-23	5
4	4-5	4	8	4	4	7-9	4	6	6-7	10-11	16-19	4
3	2-3	3	7	3	3	5-6	2-3	5	3-5	9	12-15	3
2	1	2	6		1-2	3-4	1	4	1-2	8	8-11	2
1	0	1		2	0	1-2	0	3	0	7	4-7	1
0		0	5	1		0		2		5-6	0-3	0

Chart IX B. Wechsler-Bellevue Scattergram of Johnny

tests treating nonverbal ability. Both do relatively well on the Picture Arrangement, Picture Completion, and Object Assembly, and both fall down on the Block Design and Digit Symbols. In this instance, the greater scatter occurs in Johnny's performance, where his poorest score nets him only 4 on the weighted scale and his two best give him 11

points each. It is interesting that here again there are certain, almost uncanny, similarities between some of the boys'
remarks. For example, on number 15 on the Picture Completion, both detect a minute gap between the man's hand
and the cane he is supposed to be holding, commenting that
therefore the picture is wrong because "the man is not holding his cane."

Evaluation of Material from Projective Techniques:
Many striking differences between the boys appear on
the projective tests. Their intellectual similarity in the sense
of their level of intelligence gives no clue to the different
types of living and the different processes of psychological
growth which are taking place in each. On the Rorschach,
Tommy shows, for example, an almost dazzling brilliant
imaginative record. His fantasy life is rich and absorbing.
Three-quarters of his energy, one would say, is spent in the
company of imaginary playmates. The symbolism of religion, pirates, confederate soldiers are to him equally enter-
taining. The counterpart of this, or the defects of these
qualities lie in the tendency of a child to shut himself off
completely in this easily manipulated world of fantasy, to
avoid rather than to face the problems which emerge in
everyday living. Such a child, although there is no proof
necessarily of this with Tommy, could indulge in lying because of the ease with which he fabricates. He could, if
there was no self-corrective process in growth, drift off
into a self-preoccupation of the schizoid personality in
later adolescence.

No child is emotionally mature at ten years old, but
Tommy's emotional development lags far behind his intellectual and imaginative. He does not, however, seem to be
under any emotional blocking or pressure, and he is able to

give vent to what he feels without concern.

Johnny's Rorschach tells a very different story. This boy is extremely blocked in many areas. His intellectual development is pushing him to handle problems which are in turn evoking anxiety and blocking. Unable, like Tommy, to leap off into fantasy when the going gets rough, he is much more dammed up and thwarted. The fact that such an intelligent boy failed on five of the Rorschach cards *would, in itself, raise the question of some organic factors.*

Extremely different pictures are given by both children on the Szondi Test, Johnny's reflecting greater psychological disturbance. Johnny's chief area of tension relates to his *overwhelming need for dependency* upon his mother and yet his inability to derive happiness and satisfaction from the closeness of other people. Thus there is set up an almost insoluble problem whereby an exaggerated need and the inability to satisfy it coexist within the individual. (Was Johnny by any chance a feeding problem as a child?) Tommy, on the other hand, absorbs easily and facilely the attention and love which is given him. He appears to be the much more exhibitionistic of the two from this test. He is able to express himself, his desires, and his feelings, liking to be the center of the stage. Unlike Johnny's Szondi record in which there are definite signs of pathology, Tommy's performance would fall within normal limits.

Turning now to the Drawings made by both boys, there is interesting confirmation of much that has been mentioned previously. Johnny, for example, identifies with the woman, drawing her first. The size of the female figure also is several times larger than the male. He is still oriented toward his mother and has not begun to carve out for himself the role of the growing boy. Tommy's productions illustrate his

Chart X. Szondi Scores—Johnny

	SEXUAL		PAROXYSMAL		EGO		CONTACT	
	h	**s**	**e**	**hy**	**k**	**p**	**d**	**m**
(positive pole)	I need to be loved	I need to love and act aggressively	I need to control my emotions	I need to show my emotions	I need to keep my individuality — to be apart	I need to merge into others — to expand	I am pressed to search for new objects (restlessness)	I need to enjoy and be sustained by people
	X X X X X	X X						□ □ □
	X □	X	X	X	X	X	X	X X X X
			X	X	X	X	X X	
(negative pole)	I don't want to be loved tenderly	I want to be submissive. I don't want to be aggressive	I want to let my anger out	I need to hide my emotions	I need to deny my individuality	I am unaware of my need to expand — and I do so without insight	I am pressed to stick to one object (loyalty)	I don't expect pleasure from people

Chart X. Szondi Scores—Johnny. For comparative purposes Tommy's h and m scores are indicated by squares.

Fig. XIX. "Johnny's Figure Drawings"

fantasy in an interesting way. The man for him is a confederate soldier, skillfully drawn despite its small size with
all the trappings and paraphernalia which belong on the
uniform. This is an excellent production for an eleven-year-
old. The quality of the drawing will be seen to be much
more artistic than Johnny's attempt. (Figs. XIX and XIX A)

Fig. XIX A. "Tommy's Figure Drawings"

Drawing of the Most Unpleasant Concept again illustrates the different orientation of the two children. For Tommy the most unpleasant thing he can think of is a devil coming out of a lamp, a sort of variation on the Aladdin story but nothing he has ever really experienced or actually become frightened of. For Johnny the most frightening thing is the possibility of "being attacked." (Fig. XIX B)

The Sentence Completion Test offers interesting material and sharpens the difference between the two boys. Tommy's perpetual flights into fantasy are exemplified by such answers as the following: to the sentence, Worse than being

Fig. XIX B. "Johnny's (left) and Tommy's (right) Most Unpleasant Concepts"

lonely is . . ., he replies, "*being captured by the pirates.*" Needless to say, this is not something that actually figures in his life. Whereas Johnny running head on into reality replies to the same question, "*being sad.*" Or, again, to the sentence, It hurts when . . ., Tommy replies, "*you get stabbed by an Indian,*" while Johnny adds, "*When you get a cut.*" Johnny's dependency on his mother is shown up in the fact that he must even alter the original sentence in order to have his closure make sense. To the sentence, One's closest friends can . . ., he adds, *"is your mother."* References to food are found in Johnny's record, but not in Tommy's, again reflecting a more childish dependent level.

Evaluation of the outstanding psychological characteristics of the records of both boys still leaves us with the problem of their psychological interaction as persons and the cause or effect of psychological disturbances in regard to the epilepsy of one twin. Here one passes from the recording of facts to hypotheses and speculation based on these facts.

In regard to differences and difficulties that might arise between them, it would seem that Johnny must be psychologically penalized in the sense that Tommy, with his ready escape into fantasy, will be the more lively and imaginative. He may tend to dominate simply because he is not up against the problems which face Johnny. Johnny appears definitely handicapped psychologically, both from the Szondi and the Rorschach, *in such a way as to suggest from this material that he is the twin with the clinical symptoms.*

The summary of the findings for both boys is appended here.

SUMMARY OF TEST FINDINGS

MANNER DURING TEST

Overtly Distressed	Uneasy	Relaxed, Interested	Competitive and tense	Hostile

RATE OF PERFORMANCE

Very Slow	Slow	Average	Speedy	Excessively Speedy

I.Q. (BELLEVUE-WECHSLER)

Below Average	Average	High Average	Superior	Very Superior

PRODUCTIVITY (RORSCHACH)

7* Meager	Average	22* Rich and well ordered	Rich, but chaotic	Chaotic

RELATION TO REALITY (RORSCHACH, BELLEVUE-WECHSLER, DRAWINGS)

Fanatical exactitude	Not noticeably disturbed	Firm and good	"Artistic leeway"	Loose

USUAL — UNUSUAL THOUGHT CONTENT (RORSCHACH, UNPLEASANT CONCEPT)

Stereotyped	Average	Original	Bizarre Qualities offset by other features	Bizarre

EMOTIONAL TONE (RORSCHACH, SZONDI)

Lacking, repressed	Struggling for expression	Warm, readily available	Getting out of hand	Emotions rampant

CONSTRUCTIVE FANTASY (RORSCHACH)

Absent	Average	Active	Active +	Topheavy, withdrawal

PASSIVITY — AGGRESSION (RORSCHACH, SZONDI, UNPLEASANT CONCEPT)

Hampering passivity	Insufficient drive	Sufficient drive	Aggression +	Overpowering aggression

Chart XI. Summary of Test Findings—Johnny and Tommy
(Key: Johnny - - -; Tommy—)

*Number of Rorschach responses

[II]

Are Psychogenic Factors Involved?

MEDICAL BUILDING
Main St.
Hightown

Dear Smith:

Many thanks for your report on the twins. You are quite correct, Johnny is the epileptic. Your report was most helpful to me in discussing plans for these children with their parents. A thought occurred to me in regard to Johnny's Most Unpleasant Concept. Could one say that this drawing in some way showed his fear of the epileptic attack? I would be interested to get your reaction to such a suggestion.

On the heels of this, I am sending you another patient, Mrs. Y. Z. I will make no bones about telling you that I would like to know what sort of psychological stuff she is made of. She has innumerable vague, indefinite complaints and I no sooner get one symptom cleared up than another appears. This patient is rather typical of several whom I see, and perhaps understanding her may help me with some of the others also.

Very sincerely yours,
Robert Jones, M.D.

PROFESSIONAL BUILDING
Front St.
Hightown

Dear Jones:

I am delighted with your suggestion about Johnny's Most Unpleasant Concept. The drawing really symbolizes the small boy in the grip of something that attacks him. It is this which makes his drawing so much more realistic, despite its symbolism, than that of his twin. Moreover, this threat constitutes the main reason why the world in which Johnny lives is so different from his twin's.

I am enclosing herewith the report on Mrs. Y. Z. From the psychological point of view, you were unquestionably right in your hunch that personality problems play an important part in the total picture. I have attached, as usual, a summary chart so that you may begin to build up comparisons between your respective patients.

Very sincerely yours,
John Smith, Ph.D.

PSYCHODIAGNOSTIC APPRAISAL OF MRS Y. Z.

Observation of Behavior during Testing Period: The patient seemed mildly disturbed during the testing but was quite cooperative. She spoke very readily of her symptoms and distress, and she responded without hostility or evasion to the suggestion that psychotherapy might be important for her problem.

Evaluation of Material with Reference to Intelligence: This patient has an I.Q. of 93 on the verbal Wechsler-Bellevue which puts her in the Average Group of the total population. This is a frankly mediocre performance intellectually which would make certain types of insight-giving therapy rather problematical in their success. However, it is important to notice that there is a minimum of scatter between the various subtests so her intellectual equipment is all of a piece. There is a minimum of erraticness and an underlying psychosis can be ruled out rather conclusively.

If one pays attention to the specific subtests in detail, one finds that there is an essentially childish quality to her Abstract Thinking, an inertia and passivity to her behavioral patterns, all of which reinforce the findings from the projective techniques of an extraordinarily dependent and amorphous personality. She is obviously hypochondriacally concerned with bodily symptoms, lacking drive and interest to take her out of her immediate problems.

Evaluation of Material from Projective Techniques: The Rorschach shows an obviously neurotic disturbance of deep-seated nature and of long standing. This individual's physical symptoms would, in my opinion, unquestionably be related to the inadequacy of the personality. She has extremely few resources, either from within or without, and is a prey to anxiety and a sensuous passivity which render constructive action virtually impossible.

The Szondi shows that the dynamics of the personality are that she has an overwhelming need to be loved, succored, and tended and is still in an infantile state. These passive, dependent, and receptive needs overshadow all other attempts at adjustment, holding her in their clutches.

It is obvious that somebody whose life is so unstructured and purposeless will be a prey to depression, and she will probably make futile attempts to struggle toward better adjustment without realizing the profoundly neurotic character of her difficulties.

It seems to me that this individual cries for attention psychiatrically, and, while she cannot be assessed as a good risk

Chart showing Szondi test profile scores arranged as a grid. Factor columns (with X marks indicating reactions):

SEXUAL		PAROXYSMAL		EGO		CONTACT	
h	**s**	**e**	**hy**	**k**	**p**	**d**	**m**
I need to be loved	I need to love and act aggressively	I need to control my emotions	I need to show my emotions	I need to keep my individuality — to be apart	I need to merge into others — to expand	I am pressed to search for new objects (restlessness)	I need to enjoy and be sustained by people
X X X X X	X X X	X X X X	X X	X			
I don't want to be loved tenderly	I want to be submissive. I don't want to be aggressive	I want to let my anger out	I need to hide my emotions	I need to deny my individuality	I am unaware of my need to expand —and I do so without insight	I am pressed to stick to one object (loyalty)	I don't expect pleasure from people
	X X		X X	X X X	X X		X X

Additional pole labels within the SEXUAL group: "I want to be aggressive" (s).

Chart XII. Szondi Scores—Mrs. Y. Z.

in that startling results might be expected, nonetheless I think she would be at least receptive to help so that a better adjustment could be achieved. While unfavorable, I do not consider her hopeless. Of the neurotic component in her physical disturbance there can, I think, be no doubt whatsoever.

SUMMARY OF TEST FINDINGS

MANNER DURING TEST

Overtly Distressed	Uneasy	Relaxed, Interested	Competitive and Tense	Hostile

RATE OF PERFORMANCE

Very Slow	Slow	Average	Speedy	Excessively Speedy

I.Q. (BELLEVUE-WECHSLER)

Below Average	Average	High Average	Superior	Very Superior

PRODUCTIVITY (RORSCHACH)

Meager	Average	Rich and well ordered	Rich, but chaotic	Chaotic

RELATION TO REALITY (RORSCHACH, BELLEVUE-WECHSLER, DRAWINGS)

Fanatical exactitude	Not noticeably disturbed	Firm and good	"Artistic leeway"	Loose

USUAL — UNUSUAL THOUGHT CONTENT (RORSCHACH, UNPLEASANT CONCEPT)

Stereotyped	Average	Original	Bizarre Qualities offset by other features	Bizarre

EMOTIONAL TONE (RORSCHACH, SZONDI)

Lacking, repressed	Struggling for expression	Warm, readily available	Getting out of hand	Emotions rampant

CONSTRUCTIVE FANTASY (RORSCHACH)

Absent	Average	Active	Active +	Topheavy, withdrawal

PASSIVITY — AGGRESSION (RORSCHACH, SZONDI, UNPLEASANT CONCEPT)

Hampering passivity	Insufficient drive	Sufficient drive	Aggression +	Overpowering aggression

Chart XII A. Summary of Test Findings—Mrs. Y. Z.

[III]

~~~~~~

Can This Girl be Helped
by Psychotherapy?

MEDICAL BUILDING
Main St.
Hightown

Dear Smith:

The patient I referred to you yesterday, Margaret T., is the child of some old friends of mine. Psychotherapy seems to be in the air and they consulted me as to the possibility of their daughter being helped in this way. The girl is obviously "backward," but to what extent, I do not know. Would you give me your opinion as to the chances of her success in a therapeutic venture? Frankly, is there "enough there" to justify the expense?

Cordially yours,
Robert Jones, M.D.

PROFESSIONAL BUILDING
Front St.
Hightown

Dear Jones:

The answer to your question is so definitely in the negative and the findings so straightforward and unequivocal, that this case can be covered by a very brief report.

This patient has an I.Q. of 50 on the verbal Wechsler-Bellevue, which puts her well within the mental defective group. She failed to score at all on three of the subtests, had very low scores on the other two.

As examples of the types of mistakes she makes, she finds there are three weeks in a year, does not know where London is, who wrote Hamlet, cannot think of the capital of Italy, does not know the date of Washington's birthday. She fails, of course, on all the more difficult questions which are quite meaningless to her. She can repeat only three digits forward, none backward. She fails on all the arithmetical questions and does not even know how much four dollars and five dollars are.

In terms of the Comprehension, Reasoning, and Judgment, all the questions are quite beyond her. Lost in a forest, she would "keep on going." She would "pick up the letter she finds on the street" but "would not know what to do with it."

The Rorschach shows a very tenuous hold on reality, perseveration of the organic type, complete emotional inadequacy, and lack of all critical ability. The drawings of the human figures have distinctly bizarre qualities. In the man, the eyes and mouth have been put in the stomach.

The Szondi shows a most unfavorable picture. Two main tension systems exist at the expense of all others. The Ego picture is essentially a psychotic one, with no boundaries established between the self and the world. Her behavior will be determined by unconscious projection without any insight whatsoever. Strong aggressive drives, not understood, will be producing paniclike reactions. She is virtually oblivious to other people as persons, having established no genuine inter-personal relationships.

Any form of insight therapy is simply out of the question. Whether or not she could be helped to establish some sort of connection with another human being, I do not know.

In this instance, I have enclosed the Szondi chart which will show you the distribution of "pressures." The summary chart, too, is also important. Note, on the one hand, the meager productivity and the stereotyped thinking and the lack of all constructive fantasy, at the same time the lack of adequate relationship to reality and the lack of emotional control. The total picture could hardly be called promising. I am sorry to have to make such a statement, but any softening of the appraisal would result in unrealistic handling of the case.

Very sincerely yours,
John Smith, Ph.D.

	SEXUAL		PAROXYSMAL		EGO		CONTACT	
	h	**s**	**e**	**hy**	**k**	**p**	**d**	**m**
+	I need to be loved	I need to love and act aggressively	I need to control my emotions	I need to show my emotions	I need to keep my individuality — to be apart	I need to merge into others — to expand	I am pressed to search for new objects (restlessness)	I need to enjoy and be sustained by people
scores	X X X X	X X X X X						
−	I don't want to be loved tenderly	I want to be submissive. I don't want to be aggressive	I want to let my anger out	I need to hide my emotions	I need to deny my individuality	I am unaware of my need to expand — and I do so without insight	I am pressed to stick to one object (loyalty)	I don't expect pleasure from people
scores						X X X X		

Chart XIII. Szondi Scores of Backward Child (Only particularly relevant scores given, see p. 163)

[IV]

~~~~~~

Schizophrenia or the Adolescent Struggle?

MEDICAL BUILDING
Main St.
Hightown

Dear Smith:

Thank you for your speedy appraisal of Margaret T. Sooner or later these parents had to realize what they were up against and I was very grateful for the objective findings when I discussed their daughter with them.

Now comes a problem that is perhaps the reverse of what you have just handled. The parents of this fourteen-year-old boy are worried lest some rather strange behavior at the present time may indicate a prepsychotic condition.

Cordially yours,
Robert Jones, M.D.

SUMMARY OF TEST FINDINGS

MANNER DURING TEST

Overtly Distressed	**Uneasy**	Relaxed, Interested	Competitive and Tense	Hostile

RATE OF PERFORMANCE

Very Slow	Slow	Average	Speedy	Excessively Speedy

I.Q. (BELLEVUE-WECHSLER)

I.Q. 50 Below Average	Average	High Average	Superior	Very Superior

PRODUCTIVITY (RORSCHACH)

Meager	Average	Rich and well ordered	Rich, but chaotic	Chaotic

RELATION TO REALITY (RORSCHACH, BELLEVUE-WECHSLER, DRAWINGS)

Fanatical exactitude	Not noticeably disturbed	Firm and good	"Artistic leeway"	Loose

USUAL — UNUSUAL THOUGHT CONTENT (RORSCHACH, UNPLEASANT CONCEPT)

Stereotyped	Average	Original	Bizarre Qualities offset by other features	Bizarre

EMOTIONAL TONE (RORSCHACH, SZONDI)

Lacking, repressed	Struggling for expression	Warm, readily available	Getting out of hand	**Emotions rampant**

CONSTRUCTIVE FANTASY (RORSCHACH)

Absent	Average	Active	Active +	Topheavy, withdrawal

PASSIVITY — AGGRESSION (RORSCHACH, SZONDI, UNPLEASANT CONCEPT)

Hampering passivity	Insufficient drive	Sufficient drive	Aggression +	**Overpowering aggression**

Chart XIV. Summary of Test Findings of Backward Child

PROFESSIONAL BUILDING
Front St.
Hightown

Dear Jones:

I think in this instance you may legitimately relieve the parents' anxiety as you will see from the report. My feeling in this instance is that the boy is not psychotic or prepsychotic.

Very sincerely yours,
John Smith, Ph.D.

PSYCHODIAGNOSTIC APPRAISAL OF PETER B.

Observation of Behavior during Testing Period: This boy is an odd combination of old-fashioned courtesy, "You will have to pardon my messy appearance," and modern manners, exemplified by the way he slouched in his chair in a completely free position. And while superficially he appeared at home, some underlying uneasiness can be sensed.

Evaluation of Material with Reference to Intelligence: This patient has an I.Q. of 130 on the verbal Wechsler-Bellevue which puts him in the Very Superior Group of the total population.

His performance falls into three distinct levels. His Memory for Digits is phenomenally good. His informational knowledge and arithmetical ability are good. His Abstract Thinking and Comprehension, Reasoning and Judgment fall below the level of the total score. The scatter of six points, however, is obtained from the exceptional score rather than inadequacy in any special area.

Characteristic of his whole performance was his extreme slowness. All types of decisions come very hard to him.

A breakdown of the subtests for additional diagnostic material reveals the following: On the Information his failures are mostly on the more difficult questions. This is the "normal" distribution for a fourteen-year-old. There are no suspicious gaps in ordinary, easy, matter of fact information.

In regard to Abstract Thinking, in no place does one find actual distortions of thought processes. His failures are "sensible" errors. Thus, for example, asked to define the similarity between air and water, he speaks of "we learn about them together." When he does not know the answer, he is willing to say so rather than hazard an erroneous statement.

On the Comprehension, Reasoning, and Judgment, there is a strange mixture of infantilism and a certain shrewdness. He estimates that the state requires a license before people get married because "it needs to make money." Compulsive indecision is reflected in the answer to the question regarding the finding of a letter on the street. He would "look it over very carefully in order to decide what to do," before finally coming up with the correct answer of mailing it. On the other hand, confronted with a fire in a theater, he would "yell, Fire!" an impulsive, unthinking reaction to the situation.

Of diagnostic significance here might be considered the exceptional score on the Digit Memory. Because of his capacity to withdraw completely as reflected in the projective techniques, this patient finds this task easy, being able to abstract himself from the social situation and concentrate completely on his task.

Evaluation of Material from Projective Techniques: A general characteristic pertaining to these five tests is the extreme slowness of this boy's response. On the Szondi, for instance, any kind of choice reaction is a painful one for him. On the Rorschach, although he actually perceives his response instantaneously, there is an extremely long delay before he is willing to voice it. The drawings of the man and woman show him to be painfully slow, resorting to tentative outlines before he would exert any pressure with his pencil.

The Rorschach shows this boy to be on the verge of a complete withdrawal from reality, absorbed and obsessed by his own fantasy to the point of disappearing into it. On the other hand, reality testing, when he emerges to deal with the real world around him, he is still adequate so that the description of an extremely withdrawn and schizoid individual rather than a schizophrenic one would appear to be the more valid diagnosis. Moreover, the absence of strong and destructive emotional forces, on the one hand, and his capacity for rapport with others, though tenuous and poorly developed, on the other, should be encouraging indications therapeutically.

Suggestions of feminine identification hinted at in the Rorschach and the threat which his whole psychosexual development has become can be seen in the Figure Drawings. He does not know whether his drawing is a man or a woman, and, being forced to choose, decides in favor of a woman. Drawing of the man presents an even greater problem.

The Szondi emphasizes the social maladjustment and the tremendous conflict in the Ego between his need to expand and to conform. Anxiety over masturbation is suggested. The most significant feature here, however, relates to his unhappiness, centering around his need to be loved but his inability to derive satisfaction from the attitudes of others.

It is as if he had a defeatist attitude in regard to anything that he could do in interpersonal relationships, expecting frustration and, therefore, being unwilling to allow himself emotional release.

This attitude of pessimism is confirmed in the Sentence Completion Test where one finds the sentence: The nicest thing about being a child . . . completed with word: *"nothing."* All sentences in which the word father or mother appear this boy refuses to answer. His solution for his unhappiness has been a retreat into his active fantasy, for he has discovered that he is less lonely when alone than when with others with whom he cannot interact. Worse than being lonely is . . . *"with too much of a crowd."*

I see no reason why this boy should become psychotic, but it is imperative that emotional rapport be established in a therapeutic situation as soon as possible. His intelligence and the vividness of his fantasy or inner life could be utilized to advantage once a firm emotional relationship has been established. On the other hand, if there is no therapeutic help, it is more than possible that he might vent his frustrated and desperately unhappy orientation in some anti-social mode of behavior despite his inherent mildness. The other alternative would be a further and further retreat into his own fantasy world with the increasing danger of his losing contact with reality.

A psychiatric consultation with a view to initiating treatment is indicated.

SUMMARY OF TEST FINDINGS

MANNER DURING TEST

Overtly Distressed	Uneasy	Relaxed, Interested	Competitive and Tense	Hostile

RATE OF PERFORMANCE

Very Slow	Slow	Average	Speedy	Excessively Speedy

I.Q. (BELLEVUE-WECHSLER)

Below Average	Average	High Average	Superior	Very Superior

PRODUCTIVITY (RORSCHACH)

Meager	Average	Rich and well ordered	Rich, but chaotic	Chaotic

RELATION TO REALITY
(RORSCHACH, BELLEVUE-WECHSLER, DRAWINGS)

Fanatical exactitude	Not noticeably disturbed	Firm and Good	"Artistic leeway"	Loose

USUAL — UNUSUAL THOUGHT CONTENT
(RORSCHACH, UNPLEASANT CONCEPT)

Stereotyped	Average	Original	Bizarre Qualities offset by other features	Bizarre

EMOTIONAL TONE (RORSCHACH, SZONDI)

Lacking, repressed	Struggling for expression	Warm, readily available	Getting out of hand	Emotions rampant

CONSTRUCTIVE FANTASY (RORSCHACH)

Absent	Average	Active	Active +	Topheavy, withdrawal

PASSIVITY — AGGRESSION
(RORSCHACH, SZONDI, UNPLEASANT CONCEPT)

Hampering passivity	Insufficient drive	Sufficient drive	Aggression +	Overpowering aggression

Chart XV. Summary of Test Findings—Peter B.

[V]

▰▰▰▰▰▰▰▰▰▰▰▰▰▰▰▰▰▰▰▰▰▰▰▰▰▰▰▰▰▰▰▰▰▰▰▰▰▰

Pain and Personality

MEDICAL BUILDING
Main St.
Hightown

Dear Smith:

Can you throw any light on headaches? This afternoon I saw a young women of twenty-one who gave a history of frequent, disabling migraine headaches which first appeared eleven years ago and have become worse during the past two years. They are of the typical migraine type, one-sided usually, throbbing and accompanied by nausea and lassitude. They usually last three to five days. Partial and intermittent relief is obtained by the use of codeine. The headaches are prone to occur before "important" engagements. They are unrelated to specific phases of the menstrual cycle. For as long as she can recall she has been constipated. The first two days of her menstrual flow, and often the fourth as well, are usually very uncomfortable because of cramps of sufficient severity to require codeine. She is also very irritable and fatigues readily during her menstrual period. She is prone to gain weight unless she watches her food intake.

She has been healthy and physically active. During her childhood, tonsils and adenoids were removed and a mastoidectomy performed. A "chronic" appendix was removed at fifteen and she has also had an operation for a deviated septum.

Physical examination reveals a healthy, attractive women, with no organic defects. There were no abnormal laboratory findings. She showed me a report of an electroencephalogram which had been done previously and had yielded a normal record, but showed marked muscular tension.

Any suggestions you can make will be gratefully received.

Cordially yours,
Robert Jones, M.D.

PSYCHODIAGNOSTIC APPRAISAL OF MRS. B. A.

Observation of Behavior during Testing Period: This patient presents an unusually attractive and poised appearance, takes the tests with interest, and at all points establishes excellent rapport with the examiner.

Evaluation of Material with Reference to Intelligence: Mrs. B. A. has an I.Q. of 120 on the verbal Wechsler-Bellevue which puts her in the Superior Group of the total population.

The majority of the subtests fall within close range of one another with the exception of the Arithmetic which dips sharply. Thus, we can describe this performance as one of relative uniformity with the exception of this specific area which shows a defect.

There is considerable information to be gained as inadvertently revealed by her types of failures. On the Information Test, for example, she shows herself to be someone not primarily interested in facts or in the mere acquiring of knowledge per se. Despite her college education, she shows some considerable gaps in information, not only in the technically more difficult questions but in common aspects of the world around her. Particularly striking is her failure to know the date of Washington's birthday which sometimes reflects insecurity in regard to the patient's status within her own family. She is somewhat careless and slapdash on questions where technically she knows the right answer. Thus, for example, the airplane was invented by "Frank Lloyd Wright," an error which she can, of course, correct when asked to direct critical scrutiny to it.

Although well-oriented in terms of relevant behavior in a variety of social situations, one finds here the word "*to regulate*" coming in with undue frequency. This suggests a certain fear of being spontaneous and "unregulated" and the *importance of law and order for the purpose of subduing the more spontaneous*. While at this stage of the testing procedure these are straws in the wind, they are strongly reinforced by the dynamic picture reflected in the projective techniques.

Understandably, no distortions of thought processes occur on the Similarities and there is no suggestion whatsoever of an underlying schizophrenic process. Again, two important clues emerge through wrong answers. A dog and a lion are alike because "they have teeth that bite" (disregarding the more obvious, animal). A fly and a tree are alike because "they are things that human beings *cannot control*." This latter again introduces the problem of what will happen when a thing is not controlled and the emphasis placed by this patient on the whole problem of aggression.

Her arithmetical failures suggest that in this type of activity she becomes anxious and does not really concentrate or put her mind on the task. Intellectually she is certainly equipped to do better than she does.

Evaluation of Material from Projective Techniques: The Rorschach record shows a highly imaginative and potentially gifted girl with very little indication of psychopathology. The record is one, frankly, which is atypical for patients examined in this diagnostic setting. She has a rare combination of warmth and imagination, excellent inner resources and personality integration, and the capacity to enjoy others, giving herself to them. All obvious neurotic pitfalls have been avoided, and she is well-equipped for the business of living.

It can be seen, however, from the strength of her fantasy life that the more routine and prosaic features of living will not interest her. (Compare her disregard of ordinary facts on the Information Test of the Wechsler-Bellevue.) It is probable that this is accompanied by some feelings of guilt since as a child her retreat into the more enticing world of make-believe may have been accompanied by clashes with parental authority.

The Szondi gives the first clue to an understanding of her symptoms for here one finds the area of greatest tension *to be the repression of her aggressive impulses*. While this will make her an unusually pliable and charming person to live with, she must be constantly fighting with the problem of a legitimate way to give vent to aggressive tendencies. Thus it is that even in the direct type of test the problem of "control" makes itself known. In the same way the aggressive oral characteristics of the two members of the animal species loom up sufficiently large to be considered as their common denominator. ("Teeth that bite.") It would appear also from the Szondi that there is some conflict in regard to ex-

SEXUAL / PAROXYSMAL / EGO / CONTACT

Group	Factor	Reaction	Score
SEXUAL	h	I need to be loved	X X
		I don't want to be loved tenderly	
	s	I need to love and act aggressively	
		I want to be submissive. I don't want to be aggressive	X X X X X
PAROXYSMAL	e	I need to control my emotions	
		I want to let my anger out	
	hy	I need to show my emotions	X X X
		I need to hide my emotions	X X
EGO	k	I need to keep my individuality — to be apart	X
		I need to deny my individuality	X X
	p	I need to merge into others — to expand	X X
		I am unaware of my need to expand — and I do so without insight	
CONTACT	d	I am pressed to search for new objects and be sustained (restlessness)	X X X
		I am pressed to stick to one object (loyalty)	
	m	I need to enjoy and be sustained by people	
		I don't expect pleasure from people	X X X

Chart XVI. Szondi Scores—Mrs. B. A.

SUMMARY OF TEST FINDINGS

MANNER DURING TEST

Overtly Distressed	Uneasy	Relaxed, Interested	Competitive and Tense	Hostile

RATE OF PERFORMANCE

Very Slow	Slow	Average	Speedy	Excessively Speedy

I.Q. (BELLEVUE-WECHSLER)

Below Average	Average	High Average	Superior	Very Superior

PRODUCTIVITY (RORSCHACH)

Meager	Average	Rich and well ordered	Rich, but chaotic	Chaotic

RELATION TO REALITY (RORSCHACH, BELLEVUE-WECHSLER, DRAWINGS)

Fanatical exactitude	Not noticeably disturbed	Firm but good	"Artistic leeway"	Loose

USUAL — UNUSUAL THOUGHT CONTENT (RORSCHACH, UNPLEASANT CONCEPT)

Stereotyped	Average	Original	Bizarre Qualities offset by other features	Bizarre

EMOTIONAL TONE (RORSCHACH, SZONDI)

Lacking, repressed	Struggling for expression	Warm, readily available	Getting out of hand	Emotions rampant

CONSTRUCTIVE FANTASY (RORSCHACH)

Absent	Average	Active	Active +	Topheavy, withdrawal

PASSIVITY — AGGRESSION (RORSCHACH, SZONDI, UNPLEASANT CONCEPT)

Hampering passivity	Insufficient drive	Sufficient drive	Repressed Aggression +	Overpowering aggression

Chart XVII. Summary of Test Findings—Mrs. B. A.

hibitionistic needs. She cannot quite accept her attractive self for what it is worth but may have some hangover of guilt connected with her glamorous desires. The "open" "e" is correlated with great frequency with psychosomatic symptoms. Aggression finds a substitute outlet through this means.

In the Drawing Tests her concept of the woman as an attractive individual of approximately her own age shows several items of interest. She has no feet, i.e., is not completely secure in regard to what she stands on. Moreover, the figure is drawn with a *long* skirt through which the legs show so that her conflict as to whether or not to "show off" her attractive limbs is represented.

Her concept of the Most Unpleasant Thing results in a female in the subway "restricted by the tightness of her dress." There are the heavy bands given to the arms and neck which are to emphasize the constricting (controlling) features.

Summary: This girl would appear to me to be excellent material for combined medical and psychological therapy. My feeling is that in this instance her symptoms of headache and constipation relate to the unsolved problem of adequate release of aggression.

[VI]

~~~~~~

Follow-up Material and Re-testing

MEDICAL BUILDING
Main St.
Hightown

Dear Smith:

I'm just back from a vacation and thought you would be interested in some follow-up material — on the patients I referred to you — which has come in to my office in the meantime.

The patient with headaches whom you saw for me was very quick to catch on to the idea that her personality difficulties may in some way be related to her headaches. I saw her several times alone and then with her husband. She has since written me that she has had fewer headaches and, more important, that when they do occur, she has been able to relate them to specific situations where her tenseness, as she describes it, became "a rising cumulative process." This tenseness followed frustrations and conflict situations into which she somehow maneuvered herself and which she then could neither resolve nor handle.

Considerably to my surprise, Mrs. Y. Z. has found her way to a group therapy session which is being held in one of the large hospitals near enough to where she lives so that she can make weekly excursions to attend. At the time when I made such a suggestion to her, she was tentative in her approach to it so that this is a considerable advance.

A satisfactory school has been found for Margaret T. which I am sure will save time, energy, and wear and tear in that family circle.

The psychiatric consultation confirmed your impression that

the adolescent boy, Peter B., while much in need of therapeutic help, was not schizophrenic. He is now in treatment with a woman therapist.

That's all the information I have at the present. I am looking forward to a year of active collaboration with you.

Cordially yours,
Robert Jones, M.D.

PROFESSIONAL BUILDING
Front Street
Hightown

Dear Jones:

Thanks for the follow-ups. Needless to say, I am always anxious to have this material. Exchange of this information makes our teamwork that much more satisfactory and, perhaps even more important, it is vital for any research that is done in the field of psychological testing.

You mentioned once that you would be interested in seeing raw material from a patient who had been tested twice. I don't always have such a case on hand, but yesterday I retested a girl whom I had seen two years before, just prior to her entering treatment. At this point her symptoms have disappeared and both she and her therapist feel she is ready to discontinue treatment.

This time I am not sending you a report, I am just sending the raw material from the two tests on Work Sheets so that you can make some comparisons for yourself. I don't think you should have too much trouble recognizing the charts which appear on this work sheet. The "scattergram" at the top left should be an old friend from the time we discussed the topic in "There's More to it Than the I.Q." You can check back to those charts if some of the abbreviations bother you. The same is true for the Szondi, the explanatory wording which I put in for teaching purposes has been left out, but you can compare this chart with the more detailed ones. The Rorschach, I admit, may seem strange at first, since it is not set up in terms of the Psychological Worlds which we discussed before. This is the much more usual and more concise method of scoring. You will find all the scoring symbols which are on the Work Sheet embedded in the larger charts so you won't have any difficulty in refreshing your memory.

I have also attached a *revised* Summary of Test Findings for this case. You remember, we used a slightly different version on the first cases we ever discussed. It's "revised" in order that it may be used quantitatively as well as simply at the descriptive level. You will see that it is rearranged so that it is the column to the far right, rather than the central one, which contains the optimal scores. Thus one can place an individual on a 1 to 5 point scale on all these categories, and if it is pertinent, end up with a numerical score. I have placed Miss D. on this chart, circling the scores from her first test, and putting a square around those from her second.

Let's have some of your comments!

Sincerely yours,
John Smith, Ph.D.

PROFESSIONAL BUILDING
Front Street
Hightown

Dear Jones:

I am glad that you found that an easy assignment! It is true, it is a pretty clear-cut case of improvement intellectually and emotionally. However, don't underestimate your own achievement in being able to get so much out of material summarized in this way. I am glad you called attention to the important change in the Arithmetic score and in the Comprehension; the rise in I.Q., as you say, is startling.

I agree the drawing of the woman seems to have been done by quite another person, and I am glad you notice the important introduction of all those color responses in the Rorschach record. I would also agree that they indicate that the patient has become a much warmer and more responsive person. I particularly liked your deduction that the person must have

WORK SHEET

VERBAL I. Q. 112

EWS	Info.	Comp.	Digit	Arith.	Sim.
18	25	20		14	23-24
17	24	19	17	13	21-22
16	23	18	16	12	20
15	21-22	17		11	19
14	20	16	15		17-18
13	18-19	15	14	10	16
12	17	14		9	15
11	15-16	12-13	13		13-14
10	13-14	11	12	8	12
9	12	10	11	7	11
8	10-11	9			9-10
7	9	8	10	6	8
6	7-8		9	5	7
5	6	5-6			5-6
4	4-5	4	8	4	4
3	2-3	3	7	3	3
2	1	2	6		1-2
1	0	1		2	0
0		0	5	1	

SZONDI

SEXUAL		PAROXYSMAL		EGO		CONTACT	
h	s	e	hy	k	p	d	m
		X					
		X					X
		X					X X
						X	X X
X	X	X			X	X	X X
X	X			X	X		
X	X			X			
X	X			X			
X	X						

OVER ALL EVALUATION = 17

PRODUCTIVITY	①	2	3	4	5
RELATION TO REALITY	1	②	3	4	5
THOUGHT CONTENT	1	②	3	4	5
CONSTRUCTIVE FANTASY	1	②	3	4	5
DRIVE	1	②	3	4	5
EMOTIONAL TONE	①	2	3	4	5
SOCIAL ATTITUDE	1	②	3	4	5
ANXIETY	1	②	3	4	5
I. Q. RATING	1	2	③	4	5

RORSCHACH

R 10	M 2				Fc
	FM 1	F 6			c
W% 50	m	F- 1			C'
D% 40	k	F% 70			FC
d%	K				CF
Dd% 10 S	FK				C

WORK SHEET

VERBAL I. Q. 130

EWS	Info.	Comp.	Digit	Arith.	Sim.
18	25	20		14	23-24
17	24	19	17	3	21-22
16	23	18	16	2	20
15	21-22	17		11	19
14	20	16	15		17-18
13	18-19	15	14	10	16
12	17	14		9	15
11	15-16	12-13	13		13-14
10	13-14	11	12	8	12
9	12	10	11	7	11
8	10-11	9			9-10
7	9	8	10	6	8
6	7-8	7	9	5	7
5	6	5-6			5-6
4	4-5	4	8	4	4
3	2-3	3	7	3	3
2	1	2	6		1-2
1	0	1	5	2	0
0		0		1	

SZONDI

SEXUAL		PAROXYSMAL		EGO		CONTACT	
h	s	•	hy	k	p	d	m
		X					X
		X				X	X
						X	X
X	X	X	X		X	X	X
X	X	X	X	X	X	X	
X	X		X	X		X	

OVER ALL EVALUATION = 34

PRODUCTIVITY	1	2	3	④	5
RELATION TO REALITY	1	2	③	4	5
THOUGHT CONTENT	1	2	3	④	5
CONSTRUCTIVE FANTASY	1	2	3	④	5
DRIVE	1	2	③	4	5
EMOTIONAL TONE	1	2	3	④	5
SOCIAL ATTITUDE	1	2	③	4	5
ANXIETY	1	2	3	④	5
I. Q. RATING	1	2	3	4	⑤

RORSCHACH

R	43	M	5			Fc	2
		FM	4	F	22	c	1
W%	20	m		F-		C'	
D%	58	k		F%	51	FC	4
d%	20	K				CF	3
Dd%	2	FK				c	2
S							

initially been "repressing a lot" to have so few responses on the Rorschach, and to show such strong inhibitions in the area of sexuality as shown in the Szondi.

Your question as to whether patients always improve on their second record has to be answered in the negative. Some do not improve even after years of therapy as their therapists will be the first to admit. But if you want to see an interesting change for the worse, take a look at these Rorschach responses, and my comments on them. In this instance a young woman, after having been tested in the routine manner prior to going into treatment, decided to abandon her plan. She struggled on for several years, until her emotional discomfort finally forced her to seek out the therapist she had originally consulted and again made arrangements to start psychotherapy. At this point she was retested by me. You will see that quite a lot of ground had been lost in the interval. I presented all the raw material to this therapist, who like yourself is interested in seeing what a patient actually produces, but, in addition, I went over the response on the Rorschach, card by card, highlighting the changes which I felt had occurred. Here are the two records side by side.

Comparative evaluation of material from the projective techniques

As an indication of a comparable worsening of the picture as reflected in the projectives, the Rorschach records are given response by response, with a card by card comment:

First Record	*Second Record*
CARD I	

1. Two people meeting on the street. It is raining; the pavement is shiny; it is around Christmastime. Both ladies are wrapped up warmly.

1. The X ray of the pelvis.
2. Some sort of insect with antennae and wings.

Comment: While the first answer reflects the free use of imagination and artist's sensitivity, setting the stage for a series of gifted productions, the responses in the second record are

SUMMARY OF TEST FINDINGS

MANNER DURING TEST

(1) Overly distressed	(2) Tense	(3) Indifferent	(4) Appropriate	(5) Relaxed and actively interested
(1) Hostile	(2) Uneasy			

I.Q. (Bellevue-Wechsler)

(1) Below average	(2) Average	(3) High average	(4) Superior	(5) Very superior

PRODUCTIVITY (Rorschach)

(1) Impoverished	(2) Reduced output	(3) Adequate	(4) Better than average	(5) Rich and well-ordered
	(2) Compulsive productivity			

RELATION TO REALITY (Rorschach, Bellevue-Wechsler, Drawings)

(1) Loose	(2) Lapses—together with good form	(3) Not noticeably disturbed	(4) Essentially firm	(5) Firm and good

USUAL-UNUSUAL THOUGHT CONTENT (Rorschach, Unpleasant Concept)

(1) Bizarre	(2) Tendency toward the bizarre	(3) Adequate	(4) Original trends	(5) Outstandingly original
(1) Stereotyped	(2) Tendency toward stereotypy			

CONSTRUCTIVE FANTASY (Rorschach)

(1) Absent	(2) Barely accessible	(3) Accessible	(4) Readily accessible	(5) Active but not hampering
(1) Withdrawal into fantasy				

DRIVE (Rorschach, Szondi, Unpleasant Concept)

(1) Overpowering aggression	(2) Over-aggressive	(3) Adequate	(4) Clearly sufficient	(5) Sufficient—exceptionally well-directed
(1) Hampering passivity	(2) Insufficient drive			

EMOTIONAL TONE (Rorschach, Szondi)

(1) Explosive emotions	(2) Getting out of hand	(3) Trend toward emotional expression	(4) Warmth available	(5) Warm, readily available
(1) Lacking	(2) Indicated but re-pressed emotions			

SOCIAL ATTITUDE (T. A. T.)

(1) Uncontrolled	(2) Constricted or neglected	(3) Adequate	(4) Well-regulated	(5) Free and flexible

ANXIETY

(1) Disintegrating	(2) Marked	(3) Moderate	(4) Not marked	(5) Lack of evidence of anxiety

OVER-ALL EVALUATION

(1) Markedly dis-turbed personality	(2) Less than adequate personality with some psycholog-ical problems	(3) Adequate personality	(4) Better than average function-ing personality	(5) Exceptionally well-integrated person-ality with excellent potential

Reprinted from M. Harrower

empty and anxiety-ridden. Sexual anxiety and concern are paramount. This is then superseded by a response which reflects her capacity to control her anxiety but gives evidence of no special giftedness.

First Record   *Second Record*
CARD II

1. Bears in a circus. Both have clowns' hats on. They are doing a dance; they are walking on their hind legs.

1. Two little Santa Clauses dancing, going off together. They have beards and red hats.

2. Like a shot of a woman's vagina taken directly at it, as though it were bleeding.

Comment: The first answers in both records are virtually identical. While the figures are spoken of as bears in a circus in the first and Santa Clauses in the second, they are perceptually the same; both show a liveliness and a successful integration of the emotion-arousing aspects of the situation. (The clowns' hats and the red hats are appropriately incorporated.) In the second record, however, this appropriate and well-controlled response is followed by a highly charged and sexually traumatic one; the "direct shot of the vagina bleeding" manifests again concern and anxiety which have a disruptive quality.

First Record   *Second Record*
CARD III

1. People. Two maids who work at Schrafft's. They come to the counter to pick up their trays. It is Thanksgiving time; the place is covered with decorations.

1. Two waiters bowing to each other as though they wait and also perform acts to entertain the guests.

Comment: Essentially the same type of imaginative and lively response. There is a shift of sex from maids to waiters, and the second perception lacks the successful utilization of the colorful side aspects of the blot which have been turned into Thanksgiving decorations. Whereas the first record has been, so to speak, all of a piece, with free, lively and imaginative answers, the second record indicates a fluctuation between retention of the old level and the introduction of disturbing components.

First Record	*Second Record*
	CARD IV
1. An animal rug — a bear.	1. A mouse all flopped out, squashed.

Comment: Although texture is utilized both times, the second record indicates a traumatization which is lacking in the first. Sensitivity is accepted and available at the time of the first record but it has met with crushing experiences by the time of the second.

First Record	*Second Record*
	CARD V
1. A rabbit, diving under some bushes. It is being chased.	1. Like a bat or moth.

Comment: The contrast here is between liveliness and an acceptance, so to speak, of the challenge of being chased, as opposed to a more static perception at the present time.

First Record	*Second Record*
	CARD VI
1. (No response).	1. Like a tiger rug, all flattened out. He had whiskers.

Comment: Sexuality in the first record evokes blocking and inhibitions. It is *terra incognita*. In the second record there is a repetition of the experiences of deflating or flattening; that which has been alive is now mutilated and lifeless.

First Record   *Second Record*
CARD VII

1. Two housewives, gossiping. They're leaning out of the windows. They're angry with each other. They're going to slam the windows down any moment.

1. Little church with steeple, clouds on either side.

Comment: There is a marked difference here. In the first record the identification is with women actively engaged in humanlike action; aggression is accepted but within well-controlled limits. A clear retreat is shown in the second record. The little church and steeple symbolically represent a sexual withdrawal; the clouds portray the extent to which anxiety hangs over and permeates this whole phase of her life.

First Record   *Second Record*
CARD VIII

1. Four frogs. It's raining and two frogs are holding flowers down to keep the rain off the other two.

1. Sort of a beetle.
2. Two animals walking up an icy glacier.

Comment: The first record shows a rather unusual and original constellation in which animal movement and color are used in a delicate fantasy. The animals walking up the icy glacier of the second record is just another expression of the unsatisfactoriness of her sexual and emotional life at the present time.

First Record	*Second Record*

CARD IX

1. A jazz band; people blowing trombones, others blowing horns. They're so excited; they're up in the sky — not really!	1. Little gnomes going to lick something in a bowl.

Comment: In both instances human movement is achieved in this "difficult" card. The fantasy in the first record, however, is much better developed.

First Record	*Second Record*

CARD X

1. Brilliant colors. An underwater scene. A weird monster, king of the ocean; crabs, eels, sea horses; they are looking at him. They are all going to walk through a coral arch.	1. This is a sort of a tableau; someone arranged sea objects; they are flat down on paper. Crabs, sea horses, coral.

Comment: The devitalization which has occurred here is quite fascinating. In the first record, both the brilliant coloring and the movement of the animals are accepted as part of the live situation. Now the same perception has been downgraded to be nothing more than a "tableau arranged on a paper."

It is hardly necessary to state that the second record reflects a much less healthy and a much less happy individual than did the first one. True, even in the first record one sees an individual caught up in moods, capable of "being in the sky," and also sufficiently blocked and inhibited to be without ideas in the presence of the challenge of sex; but there is a buoyancy and imagination which reflect a gifted individual who should surely have come into her own with therapeutic help. The final comment at the time of the first examination was: "A girl with

really outstanding creative and artistic ability, clearly functioning far below her capacities. A worthwhile person who needs
to become aware of her own possibilities and who needs help
in solving a hampering though not disrupting sexual problem."
Not only would it seem that this problem has not been solved
but there runs through the present record a pessimism and de-
featism which was totally lacking before.

Sincerely yours,
John Smith, Ph.D.

MEDICAL BUILDING
Main Street
Hightown

Dear Smith:

Thanks for the material on the "unimproved" patient. I
would be interested, of course, in knowing whether there was
as marked a difference in the other tests as there obviously was
even to me, a novice, in the Rorschach responses.

This time I am writing about something quite different.
When we first met, you showed me a comparison on that Summary of Test Findings of yours of the relative psychological
status of a married couple. I think you pointed out the interesting fact that the partner who seemed to be completely in
charge of the situation and the least disturbed, turned out, on
the test findings, and I assume subsequently in psychiatric
evaluation also, to be the more disturbed.

Yesterday I had in my office a young couple, and I couldn't
refrain from bringing out my inkblots and having them look
at them. I took down carefully what each of them said — the
husband, of course, was not in the room when I showed the
cards to the wife — and I have lined up the responses side by
side somewhat in the way in which you did with the two cases

tested before and after therapy. However, now I am afraid I am stuck or, rather, I don't feel confident in my judgments. Would you be good enough to react to these responses for me?

Cordially yours,
Robert Jones, M.D.

PROFESSIONAL BUILDING
Front Street
Hightown

Dear Jones:
Certainly I will react to the responses of the husband and wife, Mr. and Mrs. M. P.:

Comparative evaluation of the Rorschach responses of
Mr. and Mrs. M. P.

Mrs. M. P.   *Mr. M. P.*

CARD I

1. A winged animal.   1. A bat.
2. An insect.   2. Also reminds me of the skin.

Comment: Both individuals react first with the popular response, which may be considered an acceptable, uncontrolled reaction to the stimulus properties of Card I and to the demands of the test situation itself. Mrs. M. P. follows this with the type of response that is essentially a repetition of the first, i.e., her insect and her winged animal are perceptually alike. Mr. M. P., however, introduces in his second response, "the skin," an orientation of unexpected and unjustified passivity; preoccupation with the sensuous or the tactile alerts us to problems which he may have in the areas of sensuality and sexuality.

Mrs. M. P.   *Mr. M. P.*

CARD II

1. Two bears touching noses,   1. Female sex picture.
perhaps trying to get some-
thing to eat.

Comment: Mrs. M. P.'s response to the two animals in action,
which utilizes the whole blot, is again another popular and appropriate reaction to the stimulus properties of the card. The
oral emphasis is obvious; there is an acceptance of this need.
Moreover, there is indication of an active attempt to try to
satisfy it. This response falls short in that opportunities to
utilize color and opportunities to sublimate the more instinctual
type of reaction (with a response involving human beings, also
easily seen on Card II) are not taken advantage of. Mr. M. P.'s
response is a poor one perceptually and precipitates us immediately into his main trouble: preoccupation with unsolved
sexual conflicts. No energy is available for other types of reactions; considerable guilt is reflected in the fact that the statement is "a female sex picture"; he is unwilling to document or
be specific about his perceptual experience.

Mrs. M. P.   *Mr. M .P.*

CARD III

1. Two figures carrying some-   1. Two poodles.
thing, carrying it to another   2. Type of eccentric dance.
object.

Comment: The seeing of two figures in Card III is almost a
Rorschach "must." Mrs. M. P. shows some ambivalence in regard to her sexual role by an unwillingness to differentiate in
terms of the sex of the figures; on the other hand, they are
clearly seen moving purposefully, engaged in a specific task.
Mr. M. P.'s response of two poodles rather than two people
reflects greater immaturity, greater problems in his self-iden-

tification as a human being. His second answer, "a type of eccentric dance," has a pathologic flavor in that he finds it unnecessary to state that there are people doing the dancing.

Mrs. M. P.   *Mr. M. P.*

CARD IV

1. A snow monster with tremendous feet.

1. A type of furry, flying creature like a bat.
2. The head of a ceremonial mask, cow or horned animal.
3. Feet of the abominable snowman.

Comments: That both individuals utilized the highly unusual concept of the abominable snowman is a startling finding. For both of them, this card with explicit sexual connotation, evokes in some measure disturbing, threatening experiences. The use of the snowman rather than the monster would suggest frigidity, impotence, and inadequacy as at least a part of a sexual disturbance. Both comment on the large feet. Mr. M. P.'s additional answer of a ceremonial mask suggests an attempt to evoke magic, or magical defenses, in this disturbing area. The recurrence of "the furry, flying creature" reinforces the overpassive orientation indicated in Card I.

Mrs. M. P.   *Mr. M. P.*

CARD V

1. Like a winged insect or butterfly.
2. Female sex feeling; connotation of the female body.

1. A Bacchanalian impression of cloven hooves.
2. Upper part like antennae.
3. Two creatures, rather than a composite of one.

Comments: Mrs. M. P. here demonstrates for the first time the arousal of a feeling, mood, or impression which she cannot justify perceptually. She is anchored, however, in the reality situation by her first answer, which is the acceptable butterfly or insect. Mr. M. P.'s Bacchanalian impression is derived from cloven hooves, in itself a poor form response. It is interesting that in this card, which is minimally evocative of sexual responses, both husband and wife superimpose sexual reactions.

| *Mrs. M. P.* | *Mr. M. P.* |

CARD VI

1. This reminds me of a totem pole; something used for worshipping. It is sitting on top of a pedestal.	1. An insect of the beetle type. 2. The lower half is a hide. 3. Whiskers.

Comments: The totem pole is a frequently given, sublimated sexual response. Sexuality is dignified or elevated to the ceremonial or religious level. It would suggest that the snow monster with tremendous feet of Card IV is only part of her total responsiveness to the question of sexuality. What is lacking here is the essentially receptive or feminine orientation; there is no comment on the textural quality of the card, i.e., the "soft" aspects of sensuality. But, as might be expected, these receptive or passive sexual components are among Mr. M. P.'s repertoire — the "hide" and "whiskers" — bringing the proportion of such reactions to a questionable level.

| *Mrs. M. P.* | *Mr. M. P.* |

CARD VII

1. Like two female faces looking at each other — making faces like children do. The women are standing on tiptoe.	1. Rock formation, waterfall, chasm. 2. Female genitals.

Comments: Mrs. M. P. is able to achieve an appropriate human response to this card. True, the women are seen as still children, resorting to infantile games like making faces, but they are nonetheless striving, standing on tiptoe, reaching for something. Mr. M. P.'s responses relate exclusively to sexual symbols and overt sexual references. He cannot escape, so to speak, from this preoccupation to utilize the blots to better advantage, but the area which is to become female genitalia is essentially thought of as a rock formation and a chasm, which reflects his picture of the partner as hard and unyielding sexually. Along with the passive component referred to previously, it might well be that these responses also indicate unconscious fantasies of his own femininity.

Mrs. M. P.   *Mr. M. P.*

CARD VIII

1. Like two bears climbing up a steep wall.
2. There is a pretty use of color.
3. This is almost like candy or sherbet.

1. Two animals, small rodents.
2. This is like the trachea or esophagus.

Comments: Again Mrs. M. P. accepts without concern or evasion her own active sexual needs and the pleasures of orality. She is aware of the emotional challenge — "pretty use of color" — but does not succeed in integrating this as well as she might. Emotionally she is alert, but still somewhat immature. Mr. M. P. denies active movement to the animals he sees and is unable to react to the color challenge of the blot. The anatomical answer reflects an attempt to intellectualize threatening anxiety.

Mrs. M. P.   Mr. M. P.
CARD IX

1. Two dogs.   1. Lobster's claws.
                              2. An earth space creature.
                              3. A bone.
                              4. A head with a type of mous-
                                 tache.

Comments: Mrs. M. P.'s response here is minimal. She cannot grapple with the challenge of the colors nor achieve the
necessary integration to create human beings in meaningful
action. She is at home in the animal kingdom, finding dogs, as
was said in the Sentence Completion, "close to the type of human being I want to be." Mr. M. P.'s answers of lobster's claws
and fish bones suggest brittleness (claws are frequently associated with castration anxiety). In his "earthly space creature,"
he again shows his fear of identification with the male human
being per se, resorting to the unreality of science fiction. Even
the response of a head with a type of moustache reflects his
unwillingness to state that this is a man's head.

Mrs. M. P.   Mr. M. P.
CARD X

1. Two children having a bot-   1. Crustacea.
tle.   2. Magnified lice.
2. Two children blowing soap   3. Stags.
bubbles.   4. Worms.
3. Worms, spiders, beetles.   5. Head of a rabbit.
4. They are contented, not   6. Two bulls.
frightened children.   7. Two poodles.

Comments: Both individuals are able to respond more easily
to Card X. The animals and insects mentioned are all appropriate ones rated as popular. Mrs. M. P. reinforces the concept
of herself which she has been willing to give us all along; she

is childlike but happy, and fear is behind her. The contented children have, so to speak, achieved mastery over the frightening aspects of the world. Oral activity predominated. The only answer which deviates from the usual or accepted pattern in Mr. M. P.'s response to this card is the use of the word "lice"; the more neutral "insect" is given far more frequently. Its connotations are, of course, dirt.

The only suggestion of out-and-out pathology reflected in either record is Mr. M. P.'s avoidance of the concrete, e.g., disregard of the fact that a dance must be performed by someone or something in order to exist. By and large, however, the form level of the responses of both individuals is well within normal limits. While Mrs. M. P. appears as somewhat immature and childish, with both the assets and liabilities of this childlikeness, Mr. M. P. appears as essentially empty; he finds it impossible to identify with ordinary human beings, and there is a suggestion of unconscious feminine identification at a deep, symbolic level. The sexual act brings with it much guilt; dirt and guilt-laden fantasies are associated with it. Mrs. M. P. has a tendency to assume the more aggressive sexual role.

Keep on collecting records, you're doing fine!

Sincerely yours,
John Smith, Ph.D.

[VII]

~~~~~~

The Consultant Role

PROFESSIONAL BUILDING
Front Street
Hightown

Dear Jones:

I have been keeping track, on various odd bits of paper, of the things you wished me to exemplify when I got around to sending you another case history and another report.

The three I have assembled here before me are as follows: you want me to include more "raw material" from tests other than the Rorschach; you want me to include a case where the individual is functioning at very different levels, as reflected in the different projective techniques, and I see you have one notation here in which I should give an example of my role as *a consultant*, by which I guess you mean, a case in which the tests are to be some kind of deciding factor in regard to the kind of treatment a patient should receive.

The case of Mr. T. N. could perhaps be used in all of these ways. The patient was a gifted artist who had what was recognized as a psychotic break, and had been institutionalized. From having been completely out of contact, and almost unreachable, for over a year, he had begun to make very rapid strides and, in the opinion of some of his doctors, was quite ready to be discharged. *My role was to determine from my particular battery of tests — somewhat different from those used in the hospital — whether or not he was as well as he sometimes seemed, or whether further treatment might not be advisable within the institution for some time longer.* This was a pretty clear case of yes or no, stay or go, and I think that what you are perhaps

[282]

interested in is how the evidence is assessed in order that the psychologist may cast his vote in one direction or another.

This case is going to be helpful as far as your two other points are concerned, for there is no question about it that this patient performed at different levels. Or, let me put it differently — some of the tests picked up his improvements and his striking resources, while others seemed to tap the pathological level which had taken over so completely at the time of his breakdown.

Finally, I will be using the "raw material" from the Wechsler, TAT, Sentence Completion, and Figure Drawings, in addition to the Rorschach responses in order to present the full evidence in this case.

The only other thing I think I need to tell you is that the patient was completely cooperative during this rather unusually long testing session.

EVALUATION OF THE PSYCHOLOGICAL STATUS OF MR. T. N. FROM A BATTERY OF PSYCHOLOGICAL TESTS

1. *Responses to the Wechsler-Bellevue and a Consideration of the Subtest Performances.*

This patient has an I.Q. of 126 on the verbal Wechsler-Bellevue which puts him in the Superior group of the total population. The scattergram shows relatively even performance, that is, four of the five subtests fall within two points of each other on the weighted scale. The most deviant score, that of the Comprehension, is separated from the best achievement by four points only.

There are several encouraging features about this, the most important being the relative position of the Abstract Thinking on the scattergram. It will be seen that the Similarities along with the Arithmetic constitute his best scores. This is encouraging since, in schizophrenic patients, it is likely to be low due to bizarre or disturbed thinking.

Taking the subtests one by one, one finds that in the Information his failures for the most part relate to the more difficult questions. The one failure of the easy questions is a rather revealing one. He describes the functions of the heart as "pounding," an answer frequently given by individuals whose anxiety is a paramount symptom.

His Memory for digits forward is outstanding. He can complete all nine figures with ease. The reversal of the digits becomes more difficult. The dual task of recalling and reversing taxes him considerably.

On the Arithmetic he can handle the simple questions with great facility. More interesting, however, is the fact that having erroneously divided rather than multiplied in one of the more difficult problems, he is able to take the hint that there is something wrong with the answer he has come up with; namely, "Doesn't make sense to have one-twelfth of a man," and immediately revises his answer to come up with the correct figure.

On the Abstract Thinking there are only two places where his personal problems intervene and reduce his objectivity. Praise and punishment are alike because "they are both considered evils." The similarity between an egg and a seed, with its sexual significance, is sufficient to throw him off. Otherwise his answers are clear, straightforward, and untouched by distortion.

On the Comprehension, Reasoning, and Judgment, his problems are likely to break through in a way which the other subtests have not permitted. But his score, although it is lower than some of his other achievements, is *not in itself a seriously disturbed one*, and several of the answers are completely normal, acceptable, and routine. Thus, for example, he is able to state the reason why taxes are necessary is "to support the government"; that persons born deaf cannot speak because "they are unable to mimic sounds." On the other hand, he shows an intellectual weakening which will become much more evident in the unstructured material of the Rorschach — namely, an *inability to hold to the task in hand, the lack of critical awareness or control over inappropriate associations.* As to the question of how one would go about finding one's way out of the forest in the daytime, he starts right out with a philosophical discussion as to whether or not a sound would be heard if there were nobody there to hear it. It takes pressures to force him to complete the answer. Also, one finds here reactions which have been classified as typically adolescent, a kind of facetiousness. For example, asked why shoes are made of leather, he replies, "Because they have to do something with cowhide."

All in all this is an encouraging performance in the structured test. This patient is at the stage in his illness where within this particular test instrument he can cope in a normal, objective, and neutral way with the bulk of the material. He is sufficiently flexible to listen to the questions that are asked him and refrains, except in rare cases, from superimposing material from his own private world. He has a lively wit which has not been too greatly distorted by his illness. For example, he first defines a thermometer as "a quicksilver cigar," but is not content to let this stand without the addition of the proper interpretation.

From a study of the responses from this test alone, I would consider the patient completely fit to leave the institution.

2. *Consideration of Some of the Material From the TAT*
Card I (older woman – young man):

"Mother and son – the mother has said to him, 'Is that how anxious you are to please me, Tom?' He doesn't say anything, he's just glum."

Comment: The normal relationship (mother – son) is picked up here and no inappropriate material is introduced. The mother's remark could be interpreted in many ways, but the son's reaction is one of non-participation, lack of respect, disgruntledness.

Card II (two figures at bottom of stairway):

"I can't think. I will think of them. This reminds me, both females. This one is my wife, and the other one represents her old girl friend, Frances Porter. Just before we got married there had been a party at my mother-in-law's. The girl friend was there. She blew her stack at my wife; she lost her temper."

Comment: Characteristic of T. N.'s mental habits is to project the likenesses of *specific people* both into the completely nebulous inkblots and the TAT pictures. Such a trait usually indicates an exaggerated personal involvement in what otherwise could be more neutral material. This personal reminiscence, however, is not completely inapropos in that the figures are frequently seen in terms of some kind of aggressive action being taken by one toward the other. One wonders whether the patient was actually jealous of "the girl friend." There is something about the sentence "her old girl friend, Frances Porter" which seems to suggest he felt inferior and possibly threatened by this old friend with, incidentally, a masculine name.

Card III (the bedroom scene):

"Oh, yes! This male figure is me, myself. This woman is my wife on the thing (bed). On the last occasion in which we had sexual activity together."

Comment: Here again is a specificity that, of course, the actual pictures do not warrant. Male, female, and bed become for him without reservation, himself, his wife, at a specific time and place.

Card IV (two men):

"This is an old man and this, the young man. The old man is giving some advice to the young man, which the young man is too big a fool to understand."

Comment: This is frequently envisaged as a patient-therapist relationship and while not so explicitly stated by the patient, suggests a readiness to be receptive to advice or help, and an awareness of the fact that he cannot, at the moment, completely understand or appreciate it.

In the use of TAT stories* with neurotic patients, one is usually confronted with the opposite problem to what one has here; namely, in order to get them to admit that their stories have personal references, one reads them back and asks for further associations. Here it seems as if we should ask this patient, "Why is it necessary always to think of your personal experiences, your personal life?" The balance between objectivity and personal involvement is upset in the direction of the introjection of personal experiences at all times. One wonders if it would be possible for this imbalance to be made clear to this patient by contrasting his replies with those of persons

---

* See page 189 for other stories to these, or very similar pictures.

who do *not* feel the need to speak of their own particular and immediate experience at every turn.

3. *Consideration of the Answers to the Sentence Completion*

Few children fear . . . *the future.*

Comment: Very frequently this sentence is answered in terms of the thing which the person fears most. It is like whistling in the dark — children are stated as not fearing it. The patient, it would seem, has reached a point where he is contemplating the future with its very real problems and readjustment.

When an animal is wild . . . *it may end up being mild.*

Comment: One of T. N.'s habits of thinking is to drift into easy rhyming. Just before starting this test, he stated, "I recite it, you write it." However, one may also think that he is envisaging himself as emerging into a milder rather than a wild animal.

Compared to dogs, cats are . . . *more cleanly.*

Comment: Rather frequently given. Dogs, also, being associated more often with sexual activities.

Father should learn that . . . *crime does not pay.*

Comment: Not knowing about his relationship with the father, this is not immediately clear as it stands.

It is easy to get into trouble when . . . *you go to sleep.*

Comment: Possibly when the unconscious takes over.

No one can repair the damage caused by . . . *fools.*

Worse than being lonely is . . . *can't think of anything worse . . . being stupid.*

Comment: Schizophrenic patients frequently react to this sentence with the first part of T. N.'s answer. The loneliness and isolation which they have experienced seems to have a quality such that it makes all else pale when compared with it. On the other hand, the *being stupid*, along with the previous answer, *fools*, suggests an acceptance of, and appreciation of, good intellectual qualities.

If people only knew how much . . . *trouble I've seen.*

Comment: Probably just a fragment of the song, although with legitimate personal overtones.

Children are usually certain that . . . *everything will work out.*

Comment: Again, like the first sentence which relates to children's fears, part of T. N. hopes that things will work out for him, but the adult man may be skeptical of it.

The best of mothers may forget . . . *there's no place like home.*

Comment: Again, in a way, a cliché, but possibly suggesting that his mother did not make a "homey" home.

Too much distance lies between . . . *two points.*

Comment: Basically an evasive type of answer, at best, non-committal.

The kind of animal I would like to be . . . *is if I had to, is a human.*

Comment: It was then explained that human beings are excluded in this answer, to which he then replied . . . *a lion.* Asked why, *because he is king of the jungle.* For all his difficulties this patient will not settle for anything less than a big, powerful and well-esteemed animal.

Nothing is harder to stop than . . . *a rolling stone going downhill.*

Comment: Somewhat of a cliché type of answer, as is the next.

He couldn't bear to touch . . . *the hot stove.*

Failure may be expected when . . . *a man hesitates.*

An effeminate man may . . . *in reality be strong.*

Comment: I would rate this answer like the king of the jungle in that the patient, in reality, feels he had strength.

A mother is more likely than a father to . . . *chastise.*

Comment: The references that there have been to father and mother do not indicate closeness to either. The mother, of the two, seems to be the disciplinarian.

It hurts when . . . *you don't fit into the group.*

Comment: A realistic answer with considerable insight.

General Comment:

None of these responses are bizarre or completely inappropriate. In fact, one can say more that they show a core of psychological resources and potential health. There is insight in the awareness of his being a misfit, indications of latent strength which he sees in himself, and at least a positively oriented expectation toward better things. The very fact that certain sentences can be answered with clichés indicates, also, that the pressures from his own preoccupation with his problems are not so strong that they superimpose themselves at every chance.

4. *Comments on Figure Drawing:*

T. N.'s manner of executing these rather interesting figures was unusual. There was no organic unity to his drawing. Segments of the hands, feet, body, head, he had put on the paper in a seemingly completely random and arbitrary manner. Watching him proceed, it was impossible to get any idea what the finished product would look like.

The figure of the man is an imaginative drawing. There is great feeling of movement. It is an excellent caricature of a pianist. The figure is well spaced on the paper. All essential bodily parts are produced. None of it has a grotesque, bizarre, or psychotic quality.

5. *Consideration of the Rorschach Responses:*

CARD 1

This *is the* Democratic Party or two Democratic Parties.

The whole mass is symbolic of the Mad Party.

Also, it could be a witch doctor's mask from Africa.

A modeling form a seamstress could use for dressmaking.

Comment:

We have two types of answers here: the normal and the abnormal. Faced with the task of responding to the inkblot, most people, as we have seen, speak of a specific thing, or things,

Ignace Jan
Paderewski

which the inkblot can resemble. Thus, our patient is quite normal when he says, "This could be a witch doctor's mask from Africa" or, "I see a modeling form a seamstress could use for dressmaking." The unusual type of response, however, is one in which there is fusion of some concept, some idea, which cannot be represented visually or seen, as, for instance, the Democratic Party, and some object which may have given rise to the response, even though it is not recognized. We find, on questioning this patient, for example, that he does see a donkey, but he is not aware of it as a donkey although it has, in fact, determined the response which he gave.

CARD II

Two Scotch terriers sniffing . . . My aunt has a Scotty called "Smoky." All these red parts resemble dogs' penises, detached and scattered.

Comment:

The atypical thinking here is reflected in the "detached and scattered penises." This experience of detachment and scattering is, of course, projected into the inkblots and is part of the patient's own problem. His sexual preoccupation demands that such answers find expression whenever possible, but the disruptive force of the "scattering" must be considered an additional and disturbing element.

CARD III

There's a song, Old Black Joe, Old Black Moe, Old Black Joe.

Satyrs with cloven hooves.

A Watuse tribesman dancing around a cooking pot.

Dimitri Mitropoulos leading an or-
chestra.

Bloody kidneys. Autopsy or operating
room.

Comment:

The many human movement responses here reflect a vital
and active fantasy life. By no stretch of the imagination could
this patient be thought of as empty or psychologically barren.
Rather, one sees an overabundance of associative material and
ideation which is not held in check or controlled by more restraining mechanisms. For the first time, there is a direct response to the colored area. The "bloody kidneys" indicate the
full impact and the unrestrained response to color.

CARD IV

Also reminds me of the Giant Gulliver
in the land of Lilliput.

Fecal material; bleeding in the bowel;
tarry stools.

Italy. The Leonardo da Vinci has im-
mense decks, 521 staterooms, 1200 pass-
engers, 550 thousand gallons of seawater
purified each day.

Comment:

The response of the Giant Gulliver is another acceptable
human movement answer. There follow, however, crude, primitive and undifferentiated percepts, such as the "fecal material"
and the "bleeding bowel." Then, irrelevant associations in
which the properties of a ship, the Leonardo da Vinci, are
superimposed on the response of Italy.

CARD V

Forehead, nose, and chin of human face. What that face represents I do not know. No eyes. My father is blind to my vision. I don't see eyes, therefore, it is a blind man. It's my father.

Comment:

Here, again, is an example of the patient's weaving in and out of something he sees, and his own strange logic. There is a subtle confusion here; the face has no eyes, "therefore" the face must be that of a blind man, and since his father is "blind to my vision" (or to his point of view), "therefore" the blot is a picture of his father.

CARD VI

A penis that talks.

Comment:

This is followed by six other sexually toned answers, equally grotesque. Card VI is well known for properties which tend to produce sexual answers. However, the quality of this patient's response is undoubtedly bizarre.

CARD VII

Two mental patients with bunny ears doing bunny hops. Jones was the recreational therapist (long story about Jones).

I would say this is a decayed corpse, a decayed human corpse.

Comment:

Here, again, this patient's percepts, namely, the things he sees, and the reminiscences which are not part of the test instructions are confused. Moreover, the mental patients have "bunny ears," which leads them to do the "bunny hop," which leads to the recreational therapist who is, of course, not seen, but, once this train of thought is started, cannot be kept out. The last answer of the "decayed corpse" is a typical schizophrenic preoccupation rarely, if ever, given by nonpsychotic individuals.

CARD VIII

A corset for a middle-aged woman, but corsets are pink and this is blue, so I am color blind.

The legs and arms of Atlas holding up the world.

Comment:

There is some interesting "reasoning" here. Since the corset is blue, but should be pink, it occurs to him that he must be color blind. The legs and arms of Atlas holding up the world, since they are tiny portions of the blot in relation to the huge world, are amongst the answers which give us the feeling of how overwhelmed this patient must be at times, and how inadequate he feels to his various tasks.

CARD IX

Middle-aged matron. Very wealthy. Social dowager from Boston. Prim, proper, and pure. It is green. It should be blue for blue blood.

Pools of blood, such as you find on
the operating floor after a bloody
operation; red, orange — orange represents love for three oranges.

Comment:

Here are typical schizophrenic associations, namely, the assumption that the part of the blot in which the "middle-aged
matron" is discovered should be blue for her "blue blood." The
handling of color here is extremely crude and unmodified. The
answer "orange, love for three oranges" is another example of
telescoped thinking and the symbolic use of color.

CARD X

I'll tell you a story. First of all, love
spelled backward spells, evol, e-v-o-l,
evol, evol, evol.

The auditor proceeds to the source of
sound. He finds two bedbugs. Hearing a cockroach.

In the blue is a spider. A tarantula.
It should be black. It's like black and
blue from a bruise.

Yellow with the orange center — fried
eggs sunny-side up.

Comment:

The patient shows himself finally able to utilize color in an
appropriate way in his answer "fried eggs sunny-side up," taking the yellow part of the blot with its orange center. This is
in marked contrast, however, to the rambling beginning, the
inappropriate story, and the association of black and blue from

a bruise, because the spider seen in the blue should have been black.

In all the answers to the cards, one finds a mixture in which a healthy core of the personality is surrounded by, or embedded in, less appropriate types of experiences.

What can be learned about the patient? One would say that at the intellectual level he is a potentially productive individual whose thoughts and associations run away with him, who seems to be functioning like a machine without a governor or time-regulating mechanism. There is a lack of critical capacity, a lack of awareness of what is relevant, a confusion of various types of intellectual experiences and intellectual tasks. He seems to lack a guiding principle as to what role he should adopt while participating in this test experience. The fact that he remembers incidents and tells stories is not in itself so abnormal *as the lack of differentiating boundaries between the task that has been set and the inroad into that task of his own spontaneous variations.* He seems like an actor who cannot wait for his cues and who may be expected to give the right speech at the wrong time. Many of his plays on words could be jokes could he but handle them with perspective.

Emotionally, he shows powerful, primitive affects. Nuances of feeling are few. He is unquestionably imaginative, but, as was mentioned before, his imagination and fantasy run away with him and are not used in the service of the ego.

My recommendation, as a result of the full battery, was that it would be wiser if the patient remained in hospital for further treatment. I wonder if you would have agreed with me.

Cordially yours,
John Smith, Ph.D.

SUGGESTIONS FOR FURTHER READING

ABT, LAWRENCE E., and BELLAK, LEOPOLD: *Projective Psychology: Clinical Approaches to the Total Personality*, Grove Press, Inc., New York, 1959.

DERI, SUSAN: *Introduction to the Szondi Test*, Grune & Stratton, New York, 1949.

DEUTSCH, ALBERT, and FISHMAN, HELEN, Editors: *The Encyclopedia of Mental Health*, 6 volumes, Franklin Watts, Inc., New York, 1963.

FRANK, LAWRENCE K.: *Projective Methods*, Charles C. Thomas, Springfield, Illinois, 1948.

FREEMAN, FRANK S.: *Theory and Practice of Psychological Testing*, Holt, Rinehart, and Winston, Inc., New York, Third Edition, 1962.

GOODENOUGH, F. L.: *Measurement of Intelligence By Drawings*, World Book Company, Yonkers, New York, 1926.

HAMMER, EMANUEL F.: *Creativity: An Exploratory Investigation of the Personalities of Gifted Adolescent Artists*, Random House, Inc., New York, 1961.

HAMMER, EMANUEL F., and others: *The Clinical Application of Projective Drawings*, Charles C. Thomas, Springfield, Illinois, 1958.

HARROWER, MOLLY; ROMAN, MELVIN; VORHAUS, PAULINE; BAUMAN, G.: *Creative Variations in The Projective Techniques*, Charles C. Thomas, Springfield, Illinois, 1960.

HARROWER, MOLLY: "The Most Unpleasant Concept Test," *Journal of Clinical Psychology*, 1950; pp. 6, 213-233.

HARROWER, MOLLY: *The Practice of Clinical Psychology*, Charles C. Thomas, Springfield, Illinois, 1961.

HOLSOPPLE, JAMES QUINTER, and MIALE, FLORENCE R.: *Sentence Completion: A Projective Method For The Study Of Personality*, Charles C. Thomas, Springfield, Illinois, 1954.

KAGAN, JEROME, and LESSER, GERALD S.: *Contemporary Issues in Thematic Apperceptive Methods*, Charles C. Thomas, Springfield, Illinois, 1961.

KLOPFER, BRUNO; AINSWORTH, MARY D.; KLOPFER, WALTER G.; HOLT, ROBERT R.: *Developments in the Rorschach Technique: Technique and Theory*, Volume I, World Book Company, Yonkers, New York, 1954.

KLOPFER, BRUNO, and others: *Developments in the Rorschach Technique: Fields of Application*, Volume II, World Book Company, Yonkers, New York, 1956.

MACHOVER, KAREN: *Personality Projection in the Drawing of the Human Figure*, Charles C. Thomas, Springfield, Illinois, 1950.

PIOTROWSKI, Z. A.: *Perceptanalysis*, The Macmillan Co., New York, 1957.

RAPAPORT, DAVID: *Diagnostic Psychological Testing*, Volumes I and II, Yearbook Publishers, Inc., Chicago, Illinois, 1946.

RORSCHACH, HERMANN: *Psychodiagnostics*, Translation and English Edition by Paul Lemkau, M.D. and Bernard Kronenberg, M.D., Grune & Stratton, New York, 1942.

WEBB, WILSE B., and others: *The Profession of Psychology*, Holt, Rinehart, and Winston, Inc., New York, 1962.

WECHSLER, DAVID: *The Measurement and Appraisal of Adult Intelligence*, The Williams & Wilkins Co., Baltimore, Maryland, Fourth Edition, 1958.

Index

ABOUT THE AUTHOR

DR. MOLLY HARROWER was born in South Africa of Scotch parents and was educated in England, receiving her degree in psychology from London University in 1928 and later studying at Cambridge. She came to the United States on a fellowship from Smith College and was appointed research assistant to Professor Kurt Koffka, with whom she worked for six years, receiving her Ph.D. in 1934. During this period she also taught at Wells College and at Bedford College, University of London. Rigorously trained in experimental psychology and problems of perception, Dr. Harrower later became increasingly interested in clinical applications and undertook for the Rockefeller Foundation a project to study perception in brain-injured persons at the Montreal Neurological Institute. During World War II Dr. Harrower was concerned with large-scale screening devices, adapting the Rorschach method to group testing and evolving new procedures of her own.

Dr. Harrower has served as Consultant to the Children's Bureau, the United States Army, and the Department of State. For several years she was Research Director of the Court Intake Project in the Children's Court in New York City. For five years she was Professor of Research in Clinical Psychology in the Department of Psychiatry at Temple University Medical Center in Philadelphia. She is now Visiting Professor both in the New School for Social Research in New York and the University of Florida in Gainesville. At its inception, and for nine years, she held the position of Chairman of the Advisory Council in Psychology to the University of the State of New York. She is one of our leading clinical psychologists, having published 15 books—three of them books of poetry, and over 80 articles in professional and scientific journals. She is on the Medical Advisory Board of the National Multiple Sclerosis Society and on the Professional Board of the Academy of Religion and Mental Health.